Johann Georg Kohl

Travels in Canada and through the States of New York and Pennsylvania

Johann Georg Kohl

Travels in Canada and through the States of New York and Pennsylvania

ISBN/EAN: 9783741124099

Manufactured in Europe, USA, Canada, Australia, Japa

Cover: Foto ©ninafisch / pixelio.de

Manufactured and distributed by brebook publishing software (www.brebook.com)

Johann Georg Kohl

Travels in Canada and through the States of New York and Pennsylvania

TRAVELS IN CANADA,

AND

THROUGH THE STATES

OF

NEW YORK AND PENNSYLVANIA.

BY

J. G. KOHL,

AUTHOR OF "RUSSIA AND THE RUSSIANS," "AUSTRIA," &c. &c.

TRANSLATED BY

MRS PERCY SINNETT.

REVISED BY THE AUTHOR.

IN TWO VOLUMES.
VOL. I.

LONDON:
GEORGE MANWARING,
8, KING WILLIAM STREET, STRAND.
MDCCCLXI.

AUTHOR'S PREFACE.

A MUCH esteemed friend of mine, Mrs Percy Sinnett, thought that the English public would take an interest in a book which relates to some parts of the New World recently traversed by the Prince of Wales. She had the goodness to inform me, that she had found it worth her while to translate my *impressions de voyage* on Canada and Pennsylvania. At the same time she caused each proof-sheet to be sent to me, so that I had an opportunity of convincing myself of the most able and faithful manner in which she had interpreted the contents of the book in question.

Thinking that first impressions of foreign countries may always be of some value, I venture to offer the book to the English reader, though, having made a longer stay in the United States, having formed there many agreeable connections, and having written several other books on the same subject—published or not yet published—I would not subscribe to every sentiment contained in it.

J. G. KOHL.

Bremen, *Nov.* 21, 1860.

PREFACE

BY THE TRANSLATOR.

The numerous translations into English of the writings of M. Kohl, and the frequent notices of them in our critical journals, seem to render any further introduction superfluous—his name being nearly as well known to the reading portion of the public in England as in his own country, or, as may now be added, on the other side of the Atlantic.

The translator has, therefore, merely (at the request of the publisher) to state that the present work has been selected from those in which the author has described his extensive travels in the

North American Continent, on account of the superior and increasing interest of the subject to this country. The recent visit of the Prince of Wales to Canada will serve, it is believed, to mark the commencement of a new era in the history of that valuable portion of the British Empire,—valuable, not on account of any direct material advantage that England derives at present from the connexion, but from the bright prospect it now more than ever holds out to those who have no prospect at home but that of increasing poverty—that struggling portion of the community which often approaches so nearly the confines of what have been truly called the "dangerous classes."

Canada may be regarded in its relation to England as a happy and prosperous child, married and settled, and capable of managing its own affairs, as well as of lending a helping hand to its younger brothers and sisters; and the bonds that connect it with the mother-country are rather those of affection and respect than those of material interest; but there are, nevertheless, social benefits to an old country in seeing its youth thus renewed in its offspring, and there must be political advantage in her maintaining in the New World a counterpoise to the immense and increasing power of a people which, with all its high and admirable qualities, has not been nationally so free from reproach, or so "clear in its great office," that its gigantic advance can be watched without some feeling of apprehension mingling with our sympathy.

England is probably the only European power that could maintain its position by the side of the United States, or hold out attractions to settlers that could bear comparison with those of the great republic; but we have here the testimony of an impartial observer, that the freedom enjoyed by the inhabitants of Canada is practically much more unrestricted than that of their neighbours; that their taxation is lighter; that their independence and liberty of self-government are scarcely, if at all, less; and that no less ample provision is made for education, that first necessity of social life.

With the completion of the system of railway communication, the greatest, perhaps the only, obstacle to the progress of Canada has been removed; for whilst the severity of its climate, healthy though it be, is certainly a drawback to its attractions, the worst effect of this was the interruption it occasioned to social and commercial intercourse, and this has now happily been overcome.

Regarding the subject, therefore, as of strong and permanent interest, on which all reliable information is acceptable, the translator cannot but hope that the account of so experienced, impartial, and eminently truthful a reporter as M. Kohl will be welcomed here as it has been elsewhere.

JANE SINNETT.

London, December, 1860.

CONTENTS

OF

VOLUME I.

CHAP.		PAGE
I.	ALONG THE HUDSON	1
II.	WEST POINT	9
III.	THE POSITION OF WEST POINT	21
IV.	THE UPPER HUDSON	28
V.	IN ALBANY	33
VI.	VERMONT	42
VII.	BURLINGTON	62
VIII.	LAKE CHAMPLAIN	73
IX.	MONTREAL	85
X.	THE "ROYAL MOUNTAIN"	96
XI.	CATHOLIC INSTITUTIONS	104
XII.	THE ST LAWRENCE	122
XIII.	QUEBEC	139
XIV.	CAPE DIAMOND	144
XV.	BEAUPORT AND FALLS OF MONTMORENCY	158

CONTENTS.

CHAP.		PAGE
XVI.	THE INDIANS OF ST LORETTE	174
XVII.	THE QUEBEC SEMINARY	184
XVIII.	MISCELLANIES	195
XIX.	FROM QUEBEC TO MONTREAL	200
XX.	THE OTTAWA	211
XXI.	A PORTAGE	230
XXII.	BYTOWN OR OTTAWA	246
XXIII.	THE FALLS OF THE OTTAWA	253
XXIV.	THE LUMBER-MEN	260
XXV.	VISIT TO THE INDIANS IN THE FOREST	270
XXVI.	THE BARRACKS HILL	279
XXVII.	HOAR-FROST	286
XXVIII.	THE CATARAGUI	303
XXIX.	THE HISTORY OF A PIECE OF LAND	313
XXX.	IMMIGRANTS	321
XXXI.	THE THOUSAND ISLANDS	331

TRAVELS IN CANADA.

CHAPTER I.

ALONG THE HUDSON.

The sudden changes, and especially the sudden brightenings, of the atmosphere in this country are truly wonderful! A few hours ago it seemed as if New York and its sky were floating away together in murky cloud and storm, and now, just as I am setting off, a sudden glory lights up land and water, the clouds vanish—the houses and every object stand out in clear, sharp outline, and the deep bright blue sky, smiling like a child after a brief shower of tears, shows the beautiful shores and the silvery river stretching far away in unclouded splendour.

The Hudson looked as tempting to me as it once did to the world-renowned captain of that name, its discoverer, and I had been told that the steamer Alida would afford me the means of gratifying my wishes, but when I proceeded to the place where she was lying at anchor, I perceived that she was making no sign of preparation, and had not even begun her travelling toilette. On inquiry, I was told "Yesterday she has ceased to run."

It was the beginning of October, and travellers visiting the Hudson for its own sake were becoming scarce. Men of business indeed were still coming in crowds, but they consider the night the best time for the passage. In daylight they think they can find something better to do than to look at scenery, and they utilise their time on board the steamer by getting their sleeping done. While they are being carried from one market to another, and moon and stars are shining, they are probably dreaming, by command of Queen Mab, of dollars and cents.

As no day-boat was to be had I determined on proceeding by rail, and I did not lose much by the change, for the line runs along the very margin of the stream, and it and its beautiful valley are never out of sight. As we shot past through the last houses of one of the suburbs of New York, I saw a group of boys standing on the top of a broken fragment of rock, and amusing themselves by throwing stones at the carriages. They seemed to be experimentalizing, to try whether they could hit a train going at full speed, and the stones came whistling through the air in rapid succession. The fingers of many of the passengers itched to give the little rascals what they deserved, but how were they to be got at?

I found the company in the carriage by no means disagreeable, though they would have been among us divided into three or four classes. I did not see a single individual whose exterior was in the least offensive, and instead of the police-officers and other officials who are the plagues of Austrian railroads, there were here, running about from carriage to carriage, only little boys, who offered for sale, apples, peaches, and confectionery; a much more suitable and convenient refreshment than beer or wine, which you can hardly drink without risk of spilling it over your neighbours; or the hot coffee or soup with which you burn your mouth at the stations in Germany.

I was much interested too by the way in which the railway public was supplied with literary spiritual refreshment. The little news-boys were not content with displaying their goods to the passengers as they took their places, but shipped themselves along with us. A traveller before he is seated has little time to buy and pay for newspapers, but the probability of custom for them is much greater when all are quietly placed. Ennui too is sure to create before long an appetite for mental aliment, which is not felt in the excitement of departure.

The news-boys have, in the mean time, arranged their little stock of political, commercial, serious, and humoristic literature in some convenient corner, and then from time to time undertake an excursion through the flying community, and whenever they see anybody yawn, immediately apply the remedy; and since their goods are moderate in price, and reading is here as customary as alternate talking and sleeping among us, they generally do a good deal of business.

It is quite usual for them to bring a selection of new books with these newspapers, and they afford no contemptible assistance in the diffusion of literary productions. American books are published ready cut, and in a convenient form for a traveller's use. Even English books are not altogether as well adapted to this sort of use; and as for our German books, we get them in mere loose leaves, and then have to wait the pleasure of the binder. Here in America people expect to have no more trouble in reading a book than in smoking a cigar.

One little literary Ganymede came rushing past our carriage with flying hair, and distributing right and left a number of printed sheets that he had hanging over his arm, and threw into the laps of the passengers. I read the paper, and found that it contained a number of critical remarks, or rather panegyrics, on a certain well-known author's Travels in Africa, extracted from various periodicals. They were merely variations on the one theme, namely, that no more interesting employment could be found in the whole world than to read this gentleman's books all through, and I had scarcely got through them than the same little flying messenger appeared again at the opposite door of the carriage, but moving with rather more difficulty than before. He was bearing a pile of these African Travels, freshly bound and profusely gilt, and presenting them right and left, as he had before done the criticisms; impressing on the passengers at the same time the fact that each of these splendid volumes cost only half a dollar.

We Germans are regarded as *par excellence* a reading people, but we are apt nevertheless to find our literary food rather hard to get at. Our books are dear, often scarce, unbound and uncut, and withdraw themselves moreover far from the railways and the great lines of traffic, into comparative retirement at Leipsig and Frankfort.

In America they are continually throwing themselves in your way, and you have but to stretch out your hand to reach them. It may easily be imagined that when publishers can command the services of thousands of such active and energetic assistants as I have described, they can sell their productions at low prices, and in quantities otherwise incredible.

I had not on setting off a place near a window, but a young man, who afterwards told me he was a steamboat steward returning from California, civilly resigned his to me when I explained that I had never made the journey before; and I had then an opportunity of enjoying the beauty of the landscape.

We were passing the remarkable high precipitous rocks called the "Palisades," which extend for twenty miles along the western bank of the river. They are full of stone quarries, and a fellow-passenger informed me that the materials for the reconstruction of the Mexican fortress of San Juan de Ulloa after the French bombardment, had been taken from them, and that afterwards in the Mexican war, the Americans had found themselves shooting down their own native granite.

The Palisades occasion a slight contraction of the bed of the river, and when they cease to offer it any obstruction, it spreads out into a kind of lake called Tappan Bay, but in the wide as well as in the narrow part it is of great depth. On this account, as well as from its almost imperceptible current, it is more like an arm of the sea than a river; and for a considerable distance up, the water is salt or brackish. Several kinds of sea animals (*Cirripedia*) are found as much as seventy miles above New York, and even at West Point cover the bottoms of vessels and floating timber, as in a sea-port. Since also the river has so slight a fall, in fact almost none at all, the tide is felt two hundred miles from New York as strongly as at New York itself. It goes as far as Albany, and is there only three feet lower than at New York; so that it appears doubtful whether the Hudson falls into an arm of the sea at New York or at West Point, or even higher.

The sea-like river now contracted its channel — mountains appeared again, and when the evening was pretty far advanced we reached West Point, and a small steamer received us, and took us over to the other side.

The moon rode bright and high in the heavens, and shone down on the beautiful landscape, the richly-wooded hills, the not very numerously scattered dwellings, the lofty forest-clad shores, and the calm waters, fifty fathoms deep. How gladly would I have gone on for many miles thus, but my enjoyment of the scene was very brief. We were soon seated in a carriage, and driving up to the high plateau, on which the hotel is the only house besides the long row of buildings which constitute the celebrated Military Academy of West Point.

CHAPTER II.

WEST POINT.

TRAVELLERS in our beloved Germany may often, it seems to me, find opportunities of becoming tolerably weary of military conversation upon the buttons worn by this or that regiment, the forms of epaulettes, the facings, &c., and other minutiæ of military toilette, which are "regulation" for certain uniforms; but in America the case is different. After hearing the whole day about dollars and cents — of how much one has gained and another lost, and a third still thinks to "make," till one's ears tingle again, it is really a pleasant relief to find oneself at West Point in the company of American officers — or perhaps of British ones come over from Canada, listening to the discussions about sword-hilts and tassels, and the interesting points aforesaid, and getting rid of the never-ending talk about dollars and cents. One feels quite anxious to know whether the moustache is "regulation" in Canada; what is, in the Union, the precise form of the salute to be given by a soldier to a passing officer, and the complete description of the uniform of a grenadier from head to foot, is quite a treat. The little Military Establishment of West Point appeared to me like an oasis in the desert, and it is really in many respects unique. While I was still under the influence of this newly-discovered charm in military affairs, I took the opportunity of visiting the Educational Establishment for young American officers.

The land of this oasis belongs to the Federal Government of the United States. It owns about 3000 acres of land in the mountains round it, and has in this district not only the right of property, but also of police and jurisdiction, so that it is entirely withdrawn from the legislative influence of the State of New York. There are many such spots in various States, which are thus, for military purposes, reserved to the Federal Government.

West Point, at a position commanding the Hudson, and well adapted to fortification, played a conspicuous part in the American War; and there are here several "Revolutionary Forts," as they are called—that is, forts existing from the time of the Revolution, such as Fort Clinton, Fort Putnam, which are now indeed partly lying in ruins, but formerly, when in possession of American troops, did good service. The junction of an English army on the south of the Hudson with another on the northern half of the river was prevented by them, and several actions took place in their vicinity. A locality associated with such remembrances is specially well adapted to an Institution of which the object is to train defenders for their country; and to this is added the consideration of its fine healthful position, and the beauty of the mountain scenery around it; and the environs offer every variety of formation—plain, table-land, mountain masses, peaks, declivities, and streams—that could be desired by an instructor in military engineering.

All these circumstances probably determined the choice of West Point by the Government for the establishment of a Military School. It was begun in 1802, with very small means, and only ten cadets; but since then, and in spite of the opposition of the violent democratic party, which had to be encountered at every proposal for improvements or financial support, the revenue and the number of cadets has considerably increased.

Jefferson, Munro, and other enlightened men, supported it by their influence; and the number of cadets is at present 224, a number, however, which has been for a long time stationary, and which appears small enough, when it is considered that this is the only establishment of the kind for a country which is about as large as all Europe. The young people are of course educated at the cost of the State, and enjoy, besides, a handsome allowance of pocket-money; the cadetships are, therefore, much sought after, and every vacancy becomes the object of keen competition.

The President of the United States has ten of them in his gift; and it is, doubtless, often a matter of great perplexity how to distribute them so as to satisfy, as far as possible, his followers and dependents. The other places are divided among the members of Congress, so that every one has one appointment, and about half a dozen cadets, on the average, are taken from each State.

The Congress grants an annual sum of about 70,000 dollars for the support of this Institution, and it also derives some revenue from the 3000 acres belonging to it, and the officers of the institution, as well as the cadets, receive pay from the military chest; but every time that further advances are required, even of small sums from Congress, they are not obtained without a struggle as for life and death. The democratic party, which is averse to all military establishments, and regards even the small army of the United States as much too large and altogether superfluous, considers the school at West Point as a mere product of aristocratic luxury, and would rather do away with it altogether than give it any further support. It is sure to put its veto upon all such grants, and much difficulty is therefore experienced in effecting any improvements in the Institution, and it is necessary to be extremely moderate in all requests, in order to avoid raising an outcry in the country. "Our members of Congress are downright tyrants and misers," said a young cadet to me; "they grudge us a few dollars for the purchase of books and instruments that we really cannot do without, and our officers have to snatch every trifle from them 'as brands from the burning.'"

That may perhaps be true, but I can easily imagine that the things that I saw were not to be obtained without trouble. I saw only the results, and certainly I discovered in them no trace of parsimony; and if the means of the Institution were really so scanty as they were represented to me, they must have been wonderfully well employed. Others may have more knowledge of this subject than I have, but assuredly I have never seen any military academy that impressed me so favourably as this of West Point. The halls of instruction and dwelling-houses of the professors, the museums, arsenals, stables, &c., form a group of most tasteful and handsome buildings. Even the library has an elegant house devoted exclusively to it, and the whole establishment, in its beautiful well-wooded and park-like grounds, has the aspect of the residence of a great English nobleman. It is a hundred times pleasanter than our military schools enclosed within their high massive walls and all under one roof. It does not appear to be the custom either here or in England to concentrate much in the same building, and the separation into different portions explains in some measure the history of the Institution, and the way in which one sum after another has been wrung from the hands of Congress.

The library contains 20,000 volumes placed in a spacious temple-like rotunda, and its regulations are extremely liberal. The loan of books may sometimes be obtained from it for as much as two months, which is not the case in any other library that I am acquainted with, either in England or America. It is also open to visitors, who are in summer very numerous, partly from the attractions of the spot itself, and sometimes from their having sons and relatives in the school.

Similarly excellent accommodation is afforded for the pictures, engravings, and other examples furnished for the draughtsmen, and for the admirably executed prize-drawings of the cadets themselves. Their copies from Raphael, Horace Vernet, and other artists, really astonished me, and I doubt whether any other military academy can exhibit such specimens in the æsthetic department of art, which can only be regarded as a luxury for tacticians, engineers, &c. I was struck by the fact that all the examples and models for the use of the pupils are from France, and I was told that in the method of teaching drawing, as well as in other branches of instruction, wherever the system is not an original American one, it is taken from the French. In the earliest period of the Institution, from 1802 till about 1812, this does not seem to have been the case. General Steuben, and other Germans in the American service, were living then, and probably from their influence the Prussian system was chiefly followed; but the enormous power and success of Napoleon, the signal defeat of the Prussians in 1803, and the renown and victories of the French army, led to the introduction of the Gallic system. It is not followed slavishly, however, and the plan may on the whole be regarded as an eclectic one.

A visit to the halls in which are deposited the models and other abundantly supplied apparatus for teaching fortification, also interested me extremely, for there are here preserved many historical curiosities sent by the Federal Government, as, for example, the flags taken from those Hessian mercenaries of mournful memory, with the Hessian arms on them. There were Mexican standards too, and some most admirably cast, but badly-served, Mexican guns, of which the Americans in the last war took more than a hundred. Most of the American officers employed in that war had been educated at this Institution.

Since these last trophies have been placed here, the Mexican language—the Spanish that is—has been introduced as a subject of study, a circumstance that appears significant. It would seem to be regarded as certain that new collisions with the Spanish race, new victories over them, and new spoils and trophies, may be confidently anticipated. The German language is not taught, which surprises me a little, not only because a knowledge of it would open so many sources of excellent instruction on military subjects, but because one-third of the American army still consists of Germans.

On a model of a fortress during a siege which is displayed in one of these halls, there were formerly 20,000 very prettily executed small figures of soldiers, as all the troops engaged were thus represented; but all these figures have been in the course of years carried off by fair visitors as *souvenirs*, and most likely attached to their watch chains and worn as trinkets. I could not but acknowledge with a sigh, that it is "*tout comme chez nous.*" Glittering epaulets and slender martial figures have their attractions for republican beauties as well as for the daughters of a monarchy, and it would seem that they have here no less than 20,000 silent admirers.

Ample space and perfect order, the freshest air, and the most exquisite cleanliness, rejoiced one everywhere in the bed-rooms and sitting-rooms of the pupils. They all stood open, and might be inspected at any moment. I mention this because it might be supposed that the republican military discipline was somewhat more lax than elsewhere. This is so little the case, that some of the officers and teachers are expected every night to make unlooked-for visits from room to room, so as to exercise control over the cadets even in their sleep; and in general the treatment of the young men in their personal relations with their teachers and superiors appeared to be gentlemanly and considerate, but not less strict than with us. Should they however break any of the regulations, these young republicans are punished quite as severely as they would be in Germany. I have a whole volume of the rules and regulations of this Academy, and some of them occasioned me not a little surprise.

I attended some of the " recitations " and military exercises of the cadets, and particularly admired their proficiency in mathematics. They were all tall, fine young fellows of from 16 to 22, none younger. They wore a grey uniform with black stripes on the trowsers, and many silver buttons on their jackets, which were something like those worn by our Hussars.

In summer they occupy a camp pitched on a fine plateau in the neighbourhood, and for three or four months never come under a roof. All the instruction and all the exercises are carried on in the camp, and from this place sham military expeditions are made for the sake of practice. The season when the cadets are in camp brings many visits from parents and friends, who like to look on at the little military spectacles, so that it is regarded as a time of gaiety and recreation; and at their riding lessons, their artillery practice, &c., the young men are sure of a numerous assembly of spectators, also *comme chez nous*. The American public in general seems to be of opinion that, since it has, with whatever reluctance, put its hand in its pocket for the dollars and cents required for books and guns, it may as well, at least, have a sight for its money.

One thing I saw that certainly did not remind me of Germany, namely, a sort of retired terrace in a beautiful spot among the rocks on the banks of the Hudson, which was set apart for the young people to settle their personal differences with their fists. Duels with swords or fire-arms are forbidden here, as at every other institution of the kind, but fist-duels, though not expressly permitted, are not expressly forbidden. For those little knots and entanglements in personal intercourse, which cannot be made straight in any other way, it is thought better to wink at this method of settlement, especially as it affords an exercise of courage; in English schools similar principles are acted on. This Academy is furnished with a most able body of teachers, the "Academy Staff," and as many of my readers may be unacquainted with this remarkable and little-known Institution, I may be permitted to mention a few other particulars concerning it. There are forty-two teachers (for only

224 pupils), divided into professors and assistant professors, seven of them for mathematics, and no less than three native Frenchmen for their own language, as well as three for drawing. Many of the teachers are highly distinguished in their particular department, and some are renowned in the world as the authors of scientific works. For example, Bailey, one of the first chemists in the United States, is the professor of chemistry and geology; Bartlett, the author of widely diffused works on mechanics, optics, and acoustics, is the professor of physics; Mahan, a celebrated military writer, is the professor of engineering, &c.; the commandant and superintendent of the whole establishment, Colonel Lee, is one of the most distinguished men and officers in the United States. I believe if there were in different parts of the American Union a dozen institutions like this, they would exercise a most beneficial influence on the state of education in the country at large, for even young men who might not afterwards adopt a military life, could hardly fail to carry with them from such academies many qualities that would be highly serviceable to them in any other career. A European traveller will find few places in the United States from which he will carry away more pleasing recollections than from West Point.

CHAPTER III.

THE POSITION OF WEST POINT.

The mountain country on which you look from the heights of West Point is one of the most beautiful districts in the United States. The mountains are of very graceful forms, with many terraces and gradations, and they are covered far and wide by woods and meadows of richest verdure, through which flows majestically the broad tranquil river. These advantages are perceived at once, but the geographical and historical importance of the position is not so immediately obvious, though it is readily admitted when pointed out.

One of the principal ridges of the Appalachian system, called by the New Yorkers their Highlands, is cut through by the Hudson, and the mountains to the east and west are of precisely similar geological structure. It is evident that the same series of elevations has taken place, and that the same formations exist, from the western side of the Hudson to the mouth of the St Lawrence. Probably at one time this geological connection was also a geographical one, that is to say, the two mountain-ridges were united. At that time the waters on the northwest declivity must have flowed towards the St Lawrence and its lakes, or rather these lakes must have extended to the foot of the declivity. Only when the chasm through which the Hudson now flows was formed, did a part of the water of those lakes burst forth and find an outlet to the south, and thus constitute the present system of the Hudson and its tributaries. That this chasm was the work of the river, such as may be seen in many other passes of the Alleghanies, is more than doubtful. In the midst of the chasm the bed of the river is extremely deep, as much as 200 feet, and at the same time its current is unusually tranquil, and it glides along its whole line with a scarcely perceptible motion. In the whole 150 miles from New York to Albany, it has not a fall of more than three or four feet.

The case is quite different, not only at Niagara, where a river is cutting through a rock before our eyes, but at the many other gaps and breaks in the districts of the Susquehannah, the Delaware, and the other rivers of Eastern North America. All these rivers have a perfectly different character, and the Hudson may be said to be quite unique among them. They mostly take an excessively winding course, while the Hudson flows as straight as a canal from north to south. They are only deep at a very short distance from the sea, while the Hudson is navigable for large ships more than a hundred and fifty miles from its mouth, up to which distance the tide reaches, whilst it is never felt above 50 miles up in any of the other streams. They have almost all a deep fall and a rapid course, and form cataracts and rapids, whilst the Hudson along its whole course has neither one nor the other. Those rivers and their branches must have flowed first through the long valleys between the two Alleghany chains, but afterwards turned aside and slipped through gaps or clefts, hurrying rapidly on through beds which it is almost certain they themselves hollowed out; but the Hudson shoots like an arrow through the mountains, apparently in no way affected by their conformation, and flows among them as deep and as tranquilly as in the plain.

From all this we may, I think, conclude that the bed of the Hudson was not hollowed out by itself, but that it existed before the river. Probably some great rent or chasm was formed by volcanic forces, and then the river, or rather some little springs found their way into it, the sea entering at the same time at the opposite extremity, and both together have rather choked up than enlarged the chasm.

From these circumstances, which, as I have said, are quite exceptional on the whole eastern coast of North America, result the peculiar advantages for the harbour of New York. The Hudson appears as a canal, which, beginning at the north-west in the region near the Canadian lakes, flows right on to the Atlantic, forming a grand water communication between plain and plain. Westward and northward from Albany all is level, and to this point roads, canals, and railways may easily be led, and there intrust their treasures to the longer watery arm. The level country near Albany is only the south-eastern corner of the immense plains, which do not even terminate at the sources of the Mississippi, and which in their broad and numerous lakes possess such a system of water communication as scarcely any other country in the world can boast. They may be regarded as one connected fresh-water sea, but in its own natural outlet the St Lawrence this inner sea has hitherto had a very inconvenient connection with the ocean.

This way is too a very long one; it turns far to the north, is interrupted by rocks and rapids, and is much encumbered and deteriorated for navigation by ice.

The Hudson valley rivals the St Lawrence as a natural outlet for those plains and lakes; it is the horn of plenty, the artery through which the rivers of those regions are poured into New York. They are sent down to Albany by many channels from Ontario and Erie, and at New York they are delivered to the great reservoir the ocean.

It is the wonderful natural formation of the cleft or gate at West Point that we have to thank for the possibility of this combination. Here was the grand difficulty of the route, and human hands would never have succeeded in overcoming it in so grand a manner as nature has done. It was much more than the cutting through Mount Athos, and were the New Yorkers of the mind of the old Greeks, they might erect at this beautiful gate of their Highlands, on the summit of these Hercules Pillars, a temple to Volcano, as well as to Neptune, and celebrate here their Olympic games and their Eleusinian mysteries. But as matters stand they are rarely good enough geographers to admire specially the work of nature at this point, and to perceive its advantages—far less to offer up a portion of the wealth it brings them in sacrifices.

Immediately above West Point you enter into quite a different region of Nature. The climatic effects of the ocean cease at the New York Highlands, and are replaced by those of the interior continent, by the sky of Canada. Thus far do the winds and other weather phenomena of the north-west prevail —and thus far from the other side do the eastern clouds and fogs come up from the ocean—as well as the more equable oceanic temperature.

In winter, when the Upper Hudson is sometimes covered with ice as far as the gate of West Point, and you travel in sledges over land and water, the vessels below West Point move about freely, the streets in New York are deep in mud, and the people are rejoicing in alternate sunshine and rain.

As the atmospheric conditions so do the plants and animals of the north-west find at West Point and along the mountain-range the end of their vast territory. Very important geological differences are also found on the two sides, if not in the internal structure of the mountains, at all events, in the more modern and superficial structure of the lowlands and plains.

The ocean and continent are both in a hydrographical and commercial relation here connected and confounded together, whilst they are separated by the still in a great measure undisturbed mountain dykes.

CHAPTER IV.

THE UPPER HUDSON.

The railroad runs close to the water-side as far up as Albany, and it is an extremely pleasant and varied route. Sometimes there was between the rocks on the right and the river on the left only just room enough for our locomotive to slip through. Sometimes the line runs on dykes and bridges fairly into the water, and as the tide was in when we passed, the water was up to the level of the dykes, and it seemed as if the carriage were rolling along its surface. Sometimes the rocks opened to the right into a wide valley watered by a smaller stream, and we obtained a glimpse into the interior of the country, over meadows, swamps, wooded declivities, and here and there a little town; but the fine, broad, brimming river on our left proved the most attractive.

It was not a bright Canadian day; the clouds and mists of the ocean had forced their way through the Hercules Pillars of West Point, and hung low and heavy over the landscape. The Hudson at this part, too, again resembled an arm of the sea, and we could scarcely see the opposite shore; but it was a pleasant surprise when it sometimes emerged suddenly from the mist, and revealed a town or a headland surrounded and set in clouds. There was, of course, no lack of sails and shipping, innumerable small craft glided up and down, and vessels of considerable size were moving along with a fresh breeze and full sails, and, as if they had been at sea, without any anxious soundings; and occasionally a steam-tug would appear with a whole fleet in tow. A different method seems to be adopted by tugs from that in use with us. Instead of dragging the ships along slowly by long ropes, one after another, the steamers here have them close to her on her right and left, and moves along in the midst of them. The motive power is said to be more efficient by this method.

If only one ship is to be towed, the little tug does not take it behind her, but attaches herself to its side, so as to form an acute angle with it. Her prow seems to pierce the hull of the large vessel, as a little narval does the belly of the whale, and she rather pushes than drags it along. With wonderful rapidity too does the little snorting energetic steamer propel the unwieldy mass, like an ant running away with a twig; but it is quite natural that this river, on which steamers were first seen, should first attain to improvements in the application of their power.

Many of the villages and localities on this part of the Hudson still bear the names bestowed on them by its discoverers the Dutch, who first opened it to the world of commerce. The Dutch possessed the river and its shores about sixty years, and when the English conquered both, they changed the names of the principal places,—" New Amsterdam" became New York, and "Fort Orange" Albany; but the Dutch had sown so many little settlements over the country, and so filled it with local appellations, that it seemed impossible to root them all out from the intercourse of daily life, and they are therefore mostly still in use. One place we passed was called Rhynbeck; another, Stugoesondt; a third, Schodack; and on the other side of the river we saw Malden, Catskill, &c. Near New York are Hoboken and Brooklyn, and the beautiful and celebrated group of blue mountains that stretched northwards from West Point and to the west of the river bears still its old name of the Catskill Mountains. The Dutch *kill*, or spring, has been retained as a generic name for little tributary streams,—such as " Norman's-kill," "Fish-kill," &c., such as the English in Australia call creeks. Besides these names, many other traces and reminiscences of the Dutch time are observable. Many landed estates are still held according to the provisions of the Dutch law; and many of the old Dutch, though now Anglicised families, are still in possession of the same lands as at that time. Such, for instance, as the family of Rensselaer—the most distinguished one in Albany and its neighbourhood—which has even retained an old Dutch rather aristocratic title through all the vicissitudes of the times. Down quite to the present day the head of that family was known as the " Patroon." There are other families of similar descent in Albany and New York, who form the kernel of society. They are the oldest families of the town, and a certain air of dignity and solid opulence distinguishes them. Dutch steadiness and English enterprise are the two chief elements in the character of the true New York merchant; and it is but lately that they have become thoroughly amalgamated. The history of the old Dutch colonies on the Hudson, and the investigation of their institutions and manners, are not objects of mere antiquarian curiosity; on the contrary, they become more important and interesting with the growth of the city, that still, in many respects, moves in the grooves of "New Amsterdam." Many of the customs and habits of the few hundred Dutchmen who first founded the city have now become those of millions. Even the Dutch language has not quite died out, but is still spoken in the old colonies of Long Island and New Jersey, and in some of the domestic circles of the above-mentioned old families. It is not, however, modern Dutch, but that which was spoken at the period of the settlement. In confirmation of this fact it was mentioned to me on good authority, that when a few years ago an American from Albany was sent as ambassador to the King of Holland, and the king at his first audience addressed him in French, the ambassador apologized for his inability to reply in that language, and spoke Dutch.

King William listened to him for a while in great surprise, and then exclaimed that he spoke exactly as people did two hundred years ago in Holland.

CHAPTER V.

IN ALBANY.

A POWERFUL steamer came to fetch us from our last railroad station over to Albany. A forest of ships of all kinds and a labyrinth of houses met our eyes as we approached it; and ships, quays, and streets were all swarming with people. What may be the present population of this great overgrown "Fort Orange" I do not know exactly, for in America it is really not worth while to burden one's memory with figures and statistical details, which are like shifting sand, and have become obsolete before you have well got them into your head. The census of last year will be found this year quite inaccurate.

The great steamer delivered us at a still more colossal hotel, which rose like a mountain not far from the shore. It was tea-time; the gong was sounding far and wide, and from all the innumerable doors and staircases came trooping the guests—ladies and gentlemen, old and young, and taking their places at some one of the long tables. The attendants at table are all of the feminine gender, and a little army of waitresses was drawn up in rank and file awaiting us. We charged into the room at speed, and in much the same tumultuous throng which in London invades the House of Lords when Her Majesty has spoken the words "Call the Commons in."

The troop of maidens was immediately in motion, pushing chairs into their places, and distributing cups of tea and coffee, sandwiches, cakes, mutton-chops, &c., with the celerity of a practised player dealing cards. To my astonishment they were commanded, and all their movements directed, by a negro, who was the head-waiter. I say to my astonishment, for, according to my notions of the prejudices of American whites against blacks, I should have thought it impossible that these white republican damsels could have been induced to submit to such a rule; though, under different circumstances, the same thing may be seen in the harems of Oriental grandees. I did see too a few little tossings of the head, and saucy faces, which reminded me of the well-known picture of a girl mocking a eunuch in a seraglio.

This negro appeared, however, born to be a head-waiter; he did the honours of the room with a skill, politeness, and tact that was really surprising. He had nothing of the noisy, obtrusive manner of head-waiters in our country. He received every guest at the door with a decorum and even dignity which was equally remote from too great obsequiousness and too much self-assertion; just the true mean which a gentleman is accustomed to observe. He seemed like some lord of the castle with a black mask on. He gave each party of guests in a few words the directions necessary for their comfort, and for their obtaining proper places, and administered, at the same time, to his subordinate ministering spirits quiet reproof, praise, or command, with the most perfect composure and tranquillity, keeping an eye too all the while on the long line of guests, and divining their wishes by their looks and gestures. Occasionally he would murmur a few words—" Don't contradict; Do as I tell you; That's right," &c., but in general he exercised his authority so quietly that it was scarcely perceptible.

After tea I walked through the town of Albany,

from one end to the other, to pay a visit to a celebrated geologist of New York, Professor Hall. A little Irish boy accompanied me, and amused me not a little. "Do you know the way to Delaware turnpike?" I asked. "I know it first-rate, sir," was the reply; he supposed I was going westward, and would like to go himself. I asked why, and what he knew of the West? "Oh, sir, the West is a good money-making place, I guess." On the way I was much struck by the extent and importance of the bookselling establishments: they were larger and filled with a greater number of handsomely bound books than I had ever seen at any in Germany, and there were at least half-a-dozen, any one of which would have been remarkable in Dresden or Munich. Albany is, it appears, a great staple place for the literary productions of New York, Boston, and other book-producing places of the Eastern States; and as the line of the great immigrant march to the West passes through it, it provides also for the spiritual wants of the wayfarers.

The appearance of the apothecaries' shops, too, both here and in New York, make it seem quite a pleasure to be ill, so gaily and elegantly were they decorated. Ours in Germany look like old chemists' laboratories. All this external splendour is however, it must be owned, somewhat deceitful. These gorgeous shops are often mere whited sepulchres, where I am told the most ignorant quacks pursue their nefarious trade.

The streets of the suburbs, as we proceeded on our walk, gradually became wider, darker, and more desolate, until at last we found ourselves in an entirely houseless region. The so-called streets terminated in broad, deep, seemingly bottomless streaks of mud, along the side of which a few boards were laid by way of pavement. You go on for miles along these planks, keeping your balance as well as you can in the darkness; right and left no houses are to be seen, and nevertheless you are still inside the town. After a while we again came to some human habitations, and I knocked at a door to ask my way, for my little Irishman, in spite of his "first-rate" knowledge, had lost his way. I had chanced upon the dwelling of a countryman; the people of the house were Germans from Cobourg, and I stopped with them for a short rest. They had lived here fourteen years, and were, they said, extremely content, though the father of the family was still only what he had been in Cobourg, a day labourer. Even as such he had been able to make some savings, and to buy a piece of land. He had a house of his own, a horse, a few cows, and pigs, and he would assuredly never have attained to such opulence as that in Cobourg. A whole quarter of Albany is inhabited by Germans, amongst whom are many Jews, and other towns and stations on the great emigrant line, Buffalo, Detroit, Chicago, &c., have districts similarly inhabited. The further you go West, the larger proportionably these districts become, until at Chicago and St Louis the towns are half German. In the Eastern States, and the cities of New England, the Germans are comparatively few.

The Americans have instituted a government office, which even we Germans, inventive as we are in that department, have not yet hit on, namely, a "State geologist." Geology is in the States a very favourite study, great attention is devoted to it, and in many cases appeal is made to the opinion of the officer, whose special duty it is also to superintend the preparation of maps of the State (*Kartographie*), and improve them to the utmost attainable degree of perfection. The geological museums too, which are found in all the capital cities, are under their care. The State of New York, in particular, has been at great expense for the cultivation of this science, and its formation and soil has been so studied and investigated in every corner, that it is one of the best known and best understood in the Union.

In no other department of nature, neither in the zoology, the botany, nor the ethnology of America, did the feeling that I was in a new continent so force itself on me as in its paleontology.

The gentleman to whom I was paying my respects on the evening in question had just completed the second part of his magnificent and admirable work on the Silurian system, and was now engaged on the third. All the shells and organic remains of a former world, which have ever been found in the State of New York—his adopted country—which are here represented with wonderful fidelity to nature, had been previously formed into a collection that for order and completeness is probably unequalled. There are several thousands of species, and yet three-fourths of them are new and peculiar to this continent; only about a fourth of them are at all known in Europe, and even these have undergone some American modification. Of each of these species Professor Hall has collected an astonishing number of individuals, in many cases thousands, and I quite revelled in the sight of all these new unaccustomed and often surprisingly elegant and fantastic forms.

We talk daily of the riches of nature and the manifold variety of her productions, but how little do we really understand her boundless profusion.

On the whole, and to some extent, we are aware of the contents of the last horn of plenty that has been poured out over the surface of the earth, but the new and noble science of paleontology enables us to perceive more and more that the outpourings of this inexhaustible horn have been countless.

Among the various scientific discoveries and results that Professor Hall has made known in the above-mentioned work, is one whose history he illustrated to me with the specimens before us. He had, namely, found among the New York fossils, first one, and then several species of viviparous mussels (*muscheln*). It had never before been an ascertained fact that there were or had been any viviparous conchylia, but on examining a large fossil mussel, he one day discovered a young one of the same species within it, and immediately conjectured that he was here introduced to a new variety in the operations of nature. He then sought for other specimens of the same species; he procured thousands and examined them all, and in great numbers of them the same phenomenon presented itself. Sometimes the young mussel was in a quite embryo state, but in many cases fully formed, and the mother had then burst and was half decayed. At length he obtained in this "testimony of the rocks" such a complete series of the conditions and stages of the existence of the young animal from the first moment to its birth and the death of the mother, that he understood the whole as well as if it had passed before his eyes.

The combination of observations which lead the palæontologist to his results are often as interesting as the chain of calculations and inferences from which the astronomer derives his knowledge; and it is no less a duty than a valuable privilege for a traveller to visit men of science living in remote parts of the civilized world, and as far as possible furnish reports of their discoveries in the often obscure field of their labours.

CHAPTER VI.

VERMONT.

As we proposed to start again at five in the morning, we were called at three; and though I was down at the first cock-crow, I found the whole house up and every room full. The luxurious reception-rooms were lit up as if for an evening party, and ladies and gentlemen in elegant travelling costume were lounging on the sofas and rocking chairs, or laying in at the blazing fires a stock of warmth for the journey on this cold October morning. Two richly-dressed ladies were even playing a polka on the piano, and a young pair in the next room were availing themselves of the music to take a few turns of a dance. It seemed as if I had come in at the last stage of an expiring ball; and yet it was only an ordinary scene at an

American hotel on the morning of departure, as I had subsequently often enough occasion to know. At half-past four the gong sounded, the black head-waiter appeared at the door of the dining-room with his fair chorus, and complimented us into our places. Early as it was, the breakfast, with all kinds of additions of pastry and savoury viands, stood in perfect readiness, and we discussed them in about two minutes, that we might have time to conquer and take possession of our places in the train. All the necessary manœuvres were punctually executed, and with the stroke of five the cars rushed off in a northerly direction. This was not exactly the plan I had proposed to myself. I had intended to go to Whitehall, at the southern end of Lake Champlain, so that I might traverse this interesting lake from one end to the other; but this plan of mine was frustrated by an official intrigue.

I had asked at the railway station for a ticket to Whitehall. "Very good, sir," said the railway official, "here is your ticket; but what do you want at Whitehall?"

"To go on by the steamer up Lake Champlain."

"Are you sure any steamer goes?"

"Why, good heavens, I have been told so often enough; and here it is printed in the Railway and

Steamboat Guide: but you yourself are the best man to tell me."

"We? oh, no! We are Vermont and New York railway men. We have nothing to do with steamers; we know nothing about them, in fact. Here, Taylor, can you tell this gentleman whether a steamer goes northward from Whitehall?"

Taylor. "Not that I know of."

Traveller. "No matter, I will go to Whitehall nevertheless. I must see Lake Champlain."

1st Vermont and New York Railway man. "Very good, sir. Here is your ticket: but take notice, if you find no such steamer as your Guide talks about; and if you have to lose your time and your money in waiting for it in this changeable cloudy weather, it's not our fault. Don't make us responsible. We have warned you!" and he washed his hands in innocency.

2nd Railway man. "But it's quite nonsense, sir, to think of seeing Lake Champlain from a steamer in such weather as this. It's a mere loss of time and money. You had much better go by us. We'll carry you in six hours right through Vermont to Burlington, and there you'll find Lake Champlain again:" and so the Yankees talked over the German; and, as I said, at five o'clock I was off for Burlington.

We passed through the pleasant country lying on either bank of the Hudson to beyond Troy. In the neighbourhood of that town, its hitherto magnificent channel decreases rapidly in breadth and depth; and whilst at Albany there was room enough and water enough for ships of the largest size, here, twenty miles higher up, there is hardly enough for the smallest. At times in the summer you may here wade through the Hudson: in fact, to speak correctly, we should say that the Hudson terminates a few miles above Troy, where two smaller rivers fall into it and feed it with fresh water. One called the Mohawk comes from the west, and the other, to which the name of the Hudson is given, from the north. This, as I have said, you can in many places drive through and walk through. We passed quite close to the confluence of these two streams, and I regretted much not being able to examine it more closely. As the streams of the Upper Hudson and the Mohawk unite here (which latter I could see falling over a rocky ledge), so do also the two principal channels of traffic for North America. Following the little Hudson to the north, and proceeding towards Lake Champlain, you find a whole web of roads, canals, and railways, by which you may reach Canada and the St Lawrence, and they mark the most direct route from the great central organ of vitality in the Union to the valley of the lower St Lawrence. A still more important web of the same kind stretches along the valley of the Mohawk to Lake Erie, Upper Canada, and the Far West; and both groups of roads begin here at the termination of the great Hudson. Among these the most famous work of human art is the Erie canal, of which I only saw the two extremities, but I heard much of this Herculean work, and especially from a gentleman in New York who had been one of the chief promoters of it, and who gave me briefly its political history. I say *political*, for almost all great public works in America, canals, railroads, bridges, &c., have to overcome not only engineering and other physical difficulties, but also the political obstacles thrown in their way. We Germans are accustomed to think that if a canal or bridge is wanted the government will perceive the necessity, take the necessary steps, and that then the work will proceed in a quiet and regular manner. But it is quite otherwise in the United States. The matter has to be discussed by a few millions of people, besides those supposed to be concerned, and is made the object of long and vehement struggles and stormy debates in the political forum.

A history of the Erie canal would throw much

light on the mode of managing these transactions in America, and we will therefore take a glance at it.

A small shallow canal from the Hudson to Lake Erie existed as early as 1806. It was only capable of carrying small vessels and light cargoes, but at the beginning of the present century a great deal was thought even of that. Since however passengers and goods came streaming from east and west in unexpected abundance (in America results often exceed all previous calculation and expectations), it began to be perceived after a few years that this Erie Canal was a very poor affair and quite unequal to the increasing traffic. It was therefore unanimously agreed, that the old work must be improved, the channel deepened, the basins enlarged, and, in fact, the canal entirely new-modelled. That the thing must be done all were agreed, but how it should be done gave occasion to great difference of opinion and the formation of various parties.

The so-called democratic party, which is always disposed to be extremely saving, and, like most very saving people, takes somewhat narrow views, and guards the national purse sometimes too jealously, was of opinion that in the execution of so colossal a work, which would cost many millions of dollars, it was necessary to go to work very cautiously.

They proposed that the canal dues should be raised a little, that the revenue resulting from the increase should be saved, and that with these savings the undertaking should be begun, and executed bit by bit. The work, they argued, would then be self-supporting, would remodel itself by its own strength, and without laying fresh burdens, and perhaps even debts, on the people.

The conservative party, on the other hand, the whigs, as they are called, who always take more comprehensive views, and are inclined to a thorough carrying out of great reforms, and mostly make a truer estimate of future events, was of opinion that the work should be executed forthwith, and with the utmost energy. Even the incurring a debt, if necessary, need not be feared. The development of the trade to the West was proceeding at such a rate, that the canal would soon be in a position not only to discharge it, but to repay twice and three times over every advance made upon it. By the method proposed by the democrats half a century might elapse before the work would be completed, and the narrow old canal would be all that time a hindrance and a fetter to trade. But let the gate only be thrown wide open, and the fertilising flood of commerce would pour in, and richly reward them for all that they might do.

The discussion was continued hotly for several years, in newspapers and periodicals, in the legislative sessions, on platforms, and at electioneering meetings. For awhile the democrats had the advantage; they terrified the people with the amount of the sum required by their opponents, and the canal works were begun in the way they had proposed. Since however they went on very slowly, since the traffic continually increased, and the wishes of the commercial world were more and more loudly expressed, public opinion begun to turn in the direction of the opposite party, and at length the whigs seized the helm. The works now went on at a great rate, money was borrowed freely, and in the course of six years, when this party remained at the head of affairs, a considerable portion of the canal was completed.

The democrats in the mean time laboured incessantly to undermine their rivals; they accused them of being spendthrifts and wasters of the public money, and prophesied the speedy ruin of the State finances. They showed that though the traffic had increased more than had been expected, the cost of the works had also exceeded all calculation, and that the burdens on the people were increasing instead of diminishing with their progress. Once more the democrats succeeded in creating an alarm, and they gained the upper hand at the elections, throwing their opponents into a minority; and by the help of this Erie Canal cry they raised themselves again into the saddle. Again for eight years the canal works now crept on at their former slow pace; as little as possible was done, that their rule might appear as easy and as economical as they could make it. The conservatives, now seeing that the commerce not only of New York but of all America would suffer, raised a general storm, and succeeded, not only by dint of arguments taken from the Erie Canal, but by the employment of every means in their power, in gaining a signal victory, and placing themselves again at the head of affairs. They even obtained at the same time some alterations in the mode of elections, and other constitutional changes in the Government of New York.

This time they remained long enough at the helm to see the great work nearly completed. There was now no longer any talk about debts; in all ways, direct and indirect, all that had been expended on the canal was returning into the pockets of the people, and, let who would be at the head of affairs, the work must be immediately completed without loss of time.

We traversed nearly the whole length of the small

State of Vermont. It is not quite 200 miles long, and about 60 miles broad, and is included between Lake Champlain on the west and the Connecticut river on the east, and corresponds pretty exactly with its eastern neighbour, New Hampshire, which stretches north and south along the Connecticut river. It may even be considered as a daughter colony of the old province, as settlers from New Hampshire crossed the Connecticut about the middle of the last century, and took up their abode in the valleys beyond the " Green Mountains," *Verts Monts;* the word is very old, and is found in the earliest French maps of the beginning of the 17th century. Very likely it was bestowed by the celebrated Canadian governor and traveller, who first discovered and navigated the lake that bears his name. As these mountains were then covered with green woods, the name must have appeared very appropriate to distinguish them from the higher mountains to the east of Connecticut, whose snow-crowned summits had been seen from the ocean, and which had been called the " White Mountains."

The whole little State of Vermont is mountainous, and resembles a Swiss canton lying at the foot of the Alps; and as the Pays de Vaud and Ticino had their powerful neighbours from whose oppressive authority they had to free themselves, so the settlers in these Green Mountains, when they had formed themselves into little communities, had to struggle against the pretensions of the mother State, and the still more powerful New York. Before the time of the American Revolution, while New York was still an English province, the inhabitants put forward claims to the territory of Vermont, asserting that it lay within the boundaries marked out for them by the English kings, and that the settlers from New Hampshire were mere unauthorised intruders, who had still to purchase from the New Yorkers the lands they had long been cultivating, as well as to subject themselves to their jurisdiction and authority. The mountaineers of Vermont now prepared to defend their natural rights, and the fields which their labour had won from the wilderness. They formed themselves into a sort of confederacy, and bid defiance at once to the claims of the New Yorkers and the grants of the English kings. Armed men crossed the frontiers from New York, and the mountaineers offered armed resistance, and many sanguinary skirmishes took place. This state of affairs lasted till the time of the American Revolution, when New York and the other former English provinces were raised into sovereign States.

The Vermonters, who, during the hostilities with

New York, had become more united, now declared themselves independent; but their sovereignty was acknowledged neither by England nor the United States. At Congress the voice of the powerful New York preponderated greatly over that of little Vermont; and for a long time the view taken by the former, that the Vermonters were mere rebels against their lawful authority, was generally received. The struggle went on with the same bloodshed as before; prisoners were made on both sides — those sent to New York being treated as rebels, and those to Vermont as rapacious invaders. Little Vermont, nevertheless, maintained its independence twenty years longer, managed its affairs without the help of Federal Government or Congress, and, to avoid New York, was even inclined to annex herself to Canada and the British; but as the number of settlers in Vermont had greatly increased since the covetous desires of New York had diminished, and Congress earnestly desired the settlement of a dispute which might be dangerous in the immediate neighbourhood of Canada, deputies from Vermont were in the year 1791 admitted to Congress, and that mountaineer confederacy received as one of the United States.* Since the restoration of tranquillity,

* Whoever desires to know more of the remarkable history of

all the valleys and slopes of Vermont have become filled with settlers. Numerous small towns have sprung up, some of which, in consequence of the increasing number of passengers to Canada, have greatly increased in proportion, but less so than in other parts of the United States. Its remote position, mountainous character, and comparative want of fertility, have prevented the rise of any of the great thronged marts which are found elsewhere. The towns are pretty, clean, peaceful little places, which contrast strikingly with the tumultuous crowded cities of the West, but each one has its own special branch of industry. The State also contains many stone quarries, and has furnished a great part of the stone from which the magnificent houses of the Broadway and the Fifth Avenue in New York have been constructed. Great blocks of marble too are obtained from these mountains, to build the palaces of the commercial aristocracy in that city and Philadelphia; and Rutland, one of the smallest of the chief towns of the State, was quite surrounded, when I saw it, by vast piles of beautiful

---

Vermont, which so strikingly resembles that of one of the Swiss cantons, may be referred to the excellent work of Professor Zadock Thompson, "History of Vermont, natural, civil, and statistical." Burlington, 1853. After I had once taken it up, I could not put it down again till I had finished it.

white freestone and many coloured marbles, some of a light bluish tint, some red, some yellow, flesh-coloured, or variegated. These marble quarries were for a long time very inadequately worked, but the railroads have had a magical effect on them; the mountains have opened their hidden treasures, and the " marble-business " is destined evidently to become one of the most important resources of the State.

Of late years, when, since the discoveries in California, people have been searching for gold in all directions, a gold-bearing district has been found in Vermont, but the discovery is of interest more in a geological than in a commercial point of view, as the precious metal is so thinly scattered that it does not pay for the working.

It is now, however, a well-ascertained fact that a peculiar thin gold-bearing formation runs like a vein, not merely through the " Green Mountains," but through the Great Eastern mountain-system of the United States. It is composed of serpentine, steatite, and soap-stone, and runs northward several hundred miles through Canada in the direction of Quebec; and southward across the Hudson to New York, and on through the Alleghanies to South Carolina. In Vermont nuggets have been found weighing several ounces (one of $8\frac{1}{2}$ ounces);

in Canada, others still larger and more numerous, which are preserved at the Geological Museum in Montreal. In South Carolina similar discoveries have been reported in the newspapers, and mention also made of silver. In Vermont it is thought that the matrix of the gold, the beautiful steatite and serpentine, will prove more useful and valuable than the metal it contains.

As we left Rutland, a young man of about 30 came and sat down by me, and began a conversation with the regulation questions. "Who are you?" "Where do you come from?" "Where are you going to?" "How do you like our country?" &c. He was a long-legged, long-armed, long-fingered, stooping figure, with head and back bent like some one going against the wind; with prominent nose, small eyes, hollow cheeks, short breath, open mouth, and lank muscular development; in short, a genuine New England Yankee of the Vermont species. When it came to my turn to put questions, he related to me with true Yankee readiness, and almost gossiping communicativeness, his whole biography. He was born in Vermont, of poor parents, and was one of nine sons, all now scattered about the world. He had worked his way through his youth, carrying on first one occupation and then another, till at last he had made his way to Iowa, in the far West, and settled as a squatter in a beautiful wilderness, where he had cut down, and grubbed up, and cleared to his heart's content, and made so many "*betterments,*" that he had obtained a right of pre-emption to a few hundred acres, and finally acquired them at a moderate price as his property. He told me all this in a rapid and impetuous manner, and with the peculiar American nasal twang, rolling off his story as if from a spinning-wheel, without ever asking whether I understood him, which indeed at last, when he got very enthusiastic in describing the fertility of his land and of the Far West in general, I did not, and only made out the often-recurring words, "crops, farms, manure, cattle, big onions, fat porkers, &c.," and with the help of a little guessing put them together, so as to make out that the crops in Iowa are enormous, the farms "first-rate," the pigs as fat as any in the whole world, and the onions as big as your head, and after seven years' planting, propagating themselves. My companion looked at the somewhat meagre swine that we saw here and there on the road, the stone quarries, and the thin covering of vegetable soil from which his countrymen earn their bread, and said the whole population could do nothing better than pack up their goods and be off to-morrow to the Far

West, where there was room enough for a hundred such States and populations as those of Vermont. He concluded by saying that he was come to see the only person he cared about in the country—his mother, who lived in Middleburg, and to bring her over to his farm in Iowa. I was about to express my approval of the good disposition herein manifested, but he gave me no time. The moment he had done speaking, he rose, stamped his feet, stretched himself, yawned a little, and then went over and sat down by a pretty young girl on the other side of the carriage, whom he had been looking at several times. She had a sweet little face and figure, and was dressed very fashionably, but I could not guess to what class of society she belonged, for these things are not so easy to make out in America as with us. Most likely she was a farmer's daughter, but she might have been of much higher rank. A wreath of Parisian artificial flowers made a very ornamental frame-work for her pretty delicate features, and she was clad from head to foot in those light rosy tints that are so much in favour with the American women. We should think they looked like butterflies, but here these gay colours are quite customary, and the fair damsels certainly know how to arrange and combine them in a very skilful and becoming manner. Rose-colour and all possible shades of red are the most prevailing, and are probably chosen to give relief to their rather pale complexions.

As my Yankee spoke in a very loud tone, I had no difficulty in hearing that he was going over his private history again for the benefit of the Vermont beauty, and he appeared to describe the fat pigs and big onions with still more animation than to me. His young countrywoman listened with evident sympathy, asked some friendly questions, which were answered with great readiness, and when he came to "the only person he cared about," exclaimed with great warmth, "You are going for your mother? Oh, that is quite right of you." I thought perhaps there might be after a time a second person that my Yankee friend "cared about." Perhaps indeed there was already. He was holding in his long lean fingers the basket in which she carried her small travelling effects, his "Guide" lay open on her lap, and when we got to Middleburg, where they were both to alight, her arm, when he had helped her out of the carriage, was drawn within his, and as they departed I perceived that he had engaged some one to carry his own trunk, and that he was laden with her shawl and mantle, umbrella, and carpet-bag. The lion seemed to be tamed, and about to bend his neck to the yoke.

It is very possible, however, that the affair was not so romantic, for, in the perfect freedom of manners that prevails between young people in America, you cannot always tell whether they have been engaged for ten years like a pair of German lovers, or whether the acquaintance dates from the last five minutes. The attentions which we suppose to indicate a tender passion may be merely such as any man here would pay to any woman; only in support of my romantic hypothesis, it may be remembered that young farmers from the Far West do often come back to the Eastern States with other views than merely to fetch their mothers, for pretty girls are very scarce in the West, and here, where all the boys of the family have generally wandered away somewhither, they are rather superabundant.

Soon after we left Middleburg four young pairs entered the carriage, appearing to form a merry party, and all eight consequently desiring to sit together. The young men in the name of their ladies drove out me and the two other men near me, and we willingly resigned our places—indeed, according to the privileges of ladies here, we could not do otherwise. But there was a poor fellow coming probably from the West, and evidently ill of a fever. He was not in quite so gay a mood as these squires of dames, on the contrary he looked very wretched and dejected. He had arranged his seat so as to make himself tolerably comfortable, and, to my great satisfaction, had at length fallen into a quiet refreshing sleep. I was in hopes that when the gay ladies noticed his illness they would respect his sleep, and they did for a moment seem inclined to do so, and looked hesitatingly at him, but when it appeared that they could find no other places they liked so well, one of the gentlemen unmercifully shook up the poor sick man and pointed to his pretty lady. The poor fellow started as if he had seen something frightful, bundled up his things as fast as he could, and moved off to find another place. It does appear to me that American ladies are rather tyrannical in the assertion of their rights. The sick man was not very likely in his feverish state to win again the sleep from which he had been so roughly awakened, especially amidst the jokes and laughter of the privileged ladies.

CHAPTER VII.

BURLINGTON.

BURLINGTON is by far the largest and most important of the small towns of Vermont. It has now above 6000 inhabitants, and there is only one among the others of which the population amounts to 4000. After the example of the United States, a smaller town, that of Montpellier, has been chosen for the seat of Government of the State, the parliament, and the authorities, though the same reason for this choice cannot exist as in New York and other large States, namely, that the multitudes of people might render the factious violence of parties dangerous to the Government. In little Burlington the "mob" can be hardly more formidable than in the still less Montpellier. Perhaps the explanation may be found in the simple fact that the rise of Burlington has been more recent, and chiefly in consequence of the steam navigation on Lake Champlain, and the greatly increased and increasing intercourse with Canada. Burlington lies in a beautiful situation on the shore of the lake, and is said to be excelled in this particular by no town in New England. The bay on which it is built forms an excellent harbour, about midway between the two extremities of the great basin, and is constantly covered with small vessels, as Burlington is the chief trading town on the lake, and the central valley of Vermont, that of Montpellier, has also here its outlet. This is the valley of the "Onion River," as it has been called, though it has now fortunately been restored to its much prettier Indian appellation, the "Winuski;" and even in this out-of-the-way little place there are commercial houses that do business to the amount of 300,000 dollars a year.

In the hotel where I quartered myself I found again, as in Albany, a negro as head-waiter. I admired the quiet and even dignified manner in which he conducted his business, and spoke of him to the proprietor, who told me that he esteemed him very highly as a thoughtful and able man. He had introduced his own system and his own regulations into his department, and was always considering how it could be still further improved.

He left him entirely to himself, the landlord said, and he had never had occasion to regret doing so.

"Is he a fugitive from the South?" I asked.

"I do not know," was the reply, "I have never asked him. His origin and antecedents are a mystery to me, but I never touch on the subject. I have another negro too, who is a real Uncle Tom, though he only performs the lowest services in the house, cutting wood, cleaning shoes, and so forth. His name is T——, would you like to see him?" We went down to the yard and found T—— busily engaged cutting wood. He spoke a little Spanish, so was, in all probability, from the South. "How do you do, T——," said the master. "Very well, sir." "You seem busy?" "Yes, I have a good deal to do to-day, and these logs are abominably tough; and then I have a number of little things to see to in the evening." "Well, take your time," said the master. "Oh yes, that's very easy to say, but I must get my work done," was the answer, "leave it to me."

"And I can leave it to him," said the landlord. "He has been a long while in my service, and I have never found any fault in him. He does his work very willingly, and if there is none for him to do he is sure to make some. He is always as quiet as you see him now, never disagrees with any one, and obeys me like a child. He is very religious, often goes to church, and has always a text at hand. I am convinced that while he is cutting his wood he is always thinking of those subjects. Many people do not believe in the possibility of an Uncle Tom, but I do; for, as I said, I have one in him."

I must own I gave some weight to this testimony, for the hotel keeper, though seemingly a good and intelligent man, was a regular Yankee, and by no means given to enthusiasm.

In the evening I went to pay some visits, taking a little boy of fourteen to show me the way. I noticed that he was chewing tobacco, and asked how long he had been addicted to that indulgence; and was told *four years,* and that he also smoked cigars. "The first time a boy gave me a bit I spit it out," he continued, "and the second too, but he said I should try again, and at last I learned to like it."

"Does your mother allow you to do this?"

"Oh, she don't know! Some people told her; and she sometimes smells me, but when she asks me I deny it right out."

"What! you tell lies?"

"Why yes, to be sure; you wouldn't have me tell her the truth? She would beat me."

"What light is that?" I asked of this hopeful youth, "is it a bonfire?"

"No; it's a house a fire I guess."

"Where is it?"

"I don't know, and I don't care. There was a ship wrecked on the lake this afternoon. The masts blew right out, and all the cargo was lost."

"Was the crew lost too?"

"I don't know, but I guess they were."

"Who does that large house belong to?"

"It did belong to Mr H., but he has gone off to the West, and has taken a lot of money with him."

"He was very rich, I suppose?"

"No; but he had a good many debts, and he didn't want to pay them, so he sold a lot of his property quietly, and then went off himself."

When I got to the house I was going to I met with a cordial reception, as did also my small and by no means elegant-looking attendant. The master of the house himself gave him a chair when he perceived that he belonged to me, and let him, in true republican fashion, make one of the company; in fact, he had entered the room just as if he thought he was, and afterwards, as it was cold, he brought his chair near the fire and made himself quite comfortable.

All this was still rather new to me. With us a

little attendant sprite of this sort would have waited outside the door or have gone into the kitchen: but I had afterwards often occasion to notice that here people of this class would, not exactly in an impudent manner, but quite unconsciously, go in everywhere with me, and introduce me, and were everywhere treated with the greatest friendliness, without any apparent effort or condescension on the part of the master of the house.

I found the ladies here engaged in needlework; they were making clothes for poor French-Canadians in the neighbouring province. These people often come from their less busy country (Lower Canada) to seek for work in Vermont, and when they do not find it, get into distress and constitute the greater part of the pauper population of the State. They also go further into New England, extend their excursions all along the shores of Lake Champlain and even to Albany, where you may see poor Canadians going about like gypsies. Some go down the Hudson to New York, where the Canadians are now greatly on the increase.

The fine large steamers on Lake Champlain, which are famous for the excellence of their structure and appointments, have usually a French Canadian crew and attendants. For attendants these polite and obliging people are especially adapted, and they are, too, willing workmen, and more modest in their pretensions than the Americans. Canadian Indians also sometimes find their way down the lake to Albany and New York; formerly it was a war path, by which, under the guidance of the French, they came down upon the south, but now they bring their little baskets, embroidered slippers, and other produce of their peaceful industry.

On the following day a friend drove me about the environs in a gig, and we also climbed the lofty tower of the university, from whose summit we looked over a magnificent panorama.

On the east we saw the whole range of the "*Verts Monts*," from which the State has its name, at a distance of from 20 to 30 miles. They rise to a height of 4000 feet, and have a very imposing aspect. Their highest points have English names, the Chin, the Nose, the Camel's Hump, and so forth.

A gentleman in Vermont told me that many lovers of Indian antiquities and history had given themselves much trouble to find out the old Indian names, and the Canadian Indians had been consulted about their traditions. Probably there are also French appellations for them. Between the mountains and the lake lies a beautiful hilly country, and beyond the lake to the west rise other high mountains, the Aderondag chain in the northern part of the State of New York. They are mostly wild and desolate in appearance, but their declivities towards the lake are cultivated and peopled. Beyond those mountains lies an extensive tableland almost 3000 feet high, which is little cultivated, and indeed known to few but hunters and fishers. It is the least visited and most thinly inhabited part of the State of New York. Here and there it presents small lakes and spots of exquisite scenery, but few travellers come to enjoy it. The great routes, that of Lake Champlain to the east, of the Mohawk, the Erie Canal, &c., on the south, and the great St Lawrence on the north, lead round this *terra incognita,* but no great road passes through it.

The land of the " Green Mountains " and that of the Aderondag range are entirely separated from each other. The long cleft of the Champlain, and its continuation to the St Lawrence, makes a striking distinction in the animals, plants, and other natural phenomena; and an entirely different Fauna and Flora is found on the western side from that of the eastern. In the former are the species of both known on the great lakes—the Ontario, Erie, &c.; but Vermont belongs in an ethnographical point of view, as well as in its natural history, as do the

New England States, to the same great province. The valley of the far-stretching lake is, to a certain extent, a continuation of that of the Hudson from south to north, and both together form a deep channel, through which southern life flows northward. I was told, for instance, that every year a very elegant kind of Colibri (humming-bird) finds its way up this route. I was told in Burlington on the 5th of October, that its golden gleam had been seen in the gardens only a week ago, and it proceeds still further northward to the St Lawrence, and even the interior of Canada, and builds its nest in the woods near Hudson's Bay, as well as on the other side of the river, as far as Nova Scotia.

That I should hear all this on the top of the tower of the University of Burlington was what I certainly had not expected, for who in Germany ever heard of such an Alma Mater? The most remarkable thing about it is its history, which may be found in the already-mentioned excellent work of Professor Thompson. It is incredible what difficulties it has had to contend with, from the first voluntary subscription at the close of the last century, when a few thousand dollars were expended in the purchase of 300,000 bricks, down to the most recent period. Half a dozen times was the little light nearly extinguished; but when the year 1833 brought the sum of 26,000 dollars, the whole was placed on a more solid footing.

Now, first, was a real library procured, and, as every professor wrote down the names of the books required for his department, the catalogue was ready even before the library.

A well-informed agent was then despatched to Europe with the money (10,000 dollars) in his pocket; and the books were then purchased at German auctions, and other places where they could be obtained advantageously. In this way a good collection of 10,000 volumes was got together— many of them still bearing the names and traces of the studies of their former owners—as Blumenbach, Jacobs, Wustemann, or Grimm.

The other scientific institutions of the little democratic State of Vermont seem also to have had a difficult and thorny path to tread. The proposal, for instance, for a grant of money for a geological survey of the country, for the appointment of a state geologist, and the preparation of a geological map, lay a long time before the State Legislature, and was rejected year after year as unnecessary, till in 1844 it was carried by a majority of 96 over 92. Probably the over-democratic constitution of Vermont is in fault, that if not popular education, at least the higher branches of science, are somewhat neglected. Of all the States of the Union Vermont has laid the broadest foundation for its political constitution. Every male of 21 years of age, and good character, is a citizen, and has the suffrage. Even negroes, who are treated here more liberally than elsewhere, have a right to vote, and no more is required of them than of the whites, though in New York and some other States they require a certain amount of property. Like individuals, corporations, as for instance towns, have all equal rights, and in this way, by pursuing the democratic principle to an extreme, they have created a kind of aristocracy. The small towns would not endure that the large ones should have any superiority over them, and towns of a hundred inhabitants, of which there are plenty in Vermont, send the same number of representatives to parliament, as, for example, Burlington, which has 6000; and consequently an inhabitant of one of those towns has 60 times the influence of one of 6000. Three of the larger towns have long since protested against this privileged inequality, but the little ones have hitherto been able to maintain their ground.

CHAPTER VIII.

LAKE CHAMPLAIN.

THE storm which had raged on Lake Champlain the day before our arrival, with such violence as to occasion some shipwrecks, had passed away when we reached it, and the little fury now lay peaceful, and smiling, and smooth as glass before us. A northwest wind, here called the "fine weather wind," had swept the sky clear of clouds, and one of the beautiful steamers, white painted and exquisitely clean, was floating like a swan on the water at Burlington, and ready to carry us away to the north. The Americans are certainly the cleanest people in the world, and a traveller who has not yet convinced himself of the fact, may do so by inspecting one of these steamers. There is not a place in them which the most elegant passenger could hesitate to enter; throughout the drawing-rooms, dining-rooms, sleeping cabins, he will find everything in the most perfect order, and brilliantly clean. The washing and bathing rooms, perfumery and hair-dressers' shops (for all these things are to be found on board), are as elegant and as well kept as in the streets of New York or Boston. They save the busy passenger much time, and allow him to attend to many things which his engrossing occupations may have left him no time for on shore.

For the enjoyment of the air and scenery too these steamers are admirably adapted. A broad high platform called the "Promenade Deck" rises in the midst, floored like a dancing-room, and affording a free view all round, and you have plenty of room for pacing about it, for these spacious vessels afford a dozen times as much room for each person as our Rhine and Danube steamers. If the wind is cold you descend to the floor below, where you find open verandas and wide balconies, and where you are protected from the wind without being hindered in the enjoyment of the scenery; or you may go lower, and find a still more sheltered seat under the colonnade that runs round the apartments of the ladies. It was really no trifling enjoyment to navigate this glorious lake in such a vessel as this.

The Frenchman Champlain was the first man

who ever fired a gun upon these waters. In 1609, when he came here from Canada, he had but three musketeers with him, but with these he struck terror into the country, and gained many victories over the wild tribes round the lake. That a man who must be regarded as the real founder of Canada, and who did more to spread European civilization and authority here than any other, should have given his name to the lake, is what no one can object to, especially as he has scarcely any other geographical monument here in the North. It is certain, however, that the Indians would long since have found a much better one.* In the language of one of the tribes it is called "*Petawa bougue,*" or "Change of land and water," which on account of its numerous islands is very suitable. Another called it "*Camaderi guarunte,*" which signifies "Mouth or Gate of the Country." The small lake connected with it to the south, which we call Lake George, the Indian natives called by a name that signifies "water attached to the great lake." The appellation "Mouth of the Country" particularly pleased me, for Lake Champlain, and its continuation, the river Richelieu, which runs into the St Lawrence, is the only natural entrance to the wide mountain district around it. It is doubt-

* There is in Canada a County of Champlain.

less an old Indian road, and in the time of the French dominion in Canada it was the mouth through which the hostile nations, the French and English, spoke to one another continually with musket and cannon thunder. For a period of more than a century, regularly every year the Canadians marched southward through the valley of the lake, to attack the British possessions and lay waste their settlements, and just as often did the British burst out through the gate to the north, at the head of the wild Iroquois, and exercise retaliation on the French. Even in the subsequent contest between England and her colonies, Lake Champlain still retained the strategic significance marked by the Indian appellation; but now for forty years past this mouth happily no longer pours forth armed soldiers and ferocious Indians, guns and blood and scalps, but steamers and locomotives and peaceful traders, and bales of goods from New York and Montreal—between which two great marts it forms the chief if not the only direct connection. On the line four hundred miles long between New York and Montreal, Lake Champlain, with the Hudson, is the principal channel of communication. It offers a hundred miles of water navigable for the largest ships; but, unfortunately, its outlet, the Richelieu, is hindered by rocks and rapids. There remained, therefore, an isthmus between the northern extremity of the lake and the St Lawrence, as between the southern and the Hudson; but canals and railways have now removed this difficulty, and made of it a single uninterrupted line.

In early, that is, pre-historic, times there was, doubtless, a period when the whole line was filled with water, and an arm of the sea passed from the St Lawrence through Lake Champlain and the Hudson, round New England, and made an island of it. The recent discovery of the skeleton of a whale on the shore of the lake puts it almost beyond a doubt that the lake was once connected with the sea, and contained sea-water as well as a kind of whale, which at the present day is found in the neighbouring seas.

Sea-shells and brackish water and the sea-tide reach, as I have said, as far up as Albany; and here on Lake Champlain I learned that seals come up the lake, along the path of the whales of old times. They come through the mighty St Lawrence, and wriggle their way among the rocks and cataracts of the Richelieu to the land-locked water, where in the winter they are often killed on the ice. I found several cases of the kind mentioned in the work of Professor Thompson before alluded to; and on talking the subject over with the captain of the steamer, I learned that it was by no means uncommon, and that two or three seals were found every year as far south as Whitehall. Between Whitehall and Albany, where the last oceanic movement from the south is felt, is a tract of about eighty miles of land; and since whales have been in our own time followed as far up the St Lawrence as Montreal, we may consider that marine animals swim nearly round the peninsula of New England, and this may perhaps explain why many of the oldest maps represent it as an island, as the first settlers supposed it to be. They heard in many places of deep navigable waters west of them, and naturally imagined a connection between them. There is also much of the islander in the character of the New England men. It is more narrow, compact, and solid than that of the people of the other States.

The whole northern part of Lake Champlain is filled with larger and smaller islands, some covered with forest, some cultivated and inhabited, and some even with little towns or villages, and others again mere rocks rising out of the water. There is one of them that bears the name of Kelton's Prize, because, according to the Americans, the commander of an English ship, during the war, took it for an enemy's vessel, and poured a broadside into it.

It was a beautiful evening on which we were steaming through these islands, the sun went down behind the Aderondag mountains in a flood of light, passing into a thousand glorious tints, till the moon rose and melted them all into her silvery splendour. The crew of our steamer consisted entirely of French-Canadians, the first whom I had seen, and they made a very favourable impression on me. They were all lively, well-behaved, agreeable men, and they still retained so much of the spirit of *la belle France*, as to find perpetual amusement in gossiping and joking with one another, when there was nothing else to be done; and the captain declared he preferred them to the Americans, who were too "independent," and would not do all kinds of work. Here also I met with Indians for the first time. As they sat in silence, wrapped in dark mantles, I took them for a group of poor German emigrants, until one of them, to whom I had in vain spoken in French, German, and English, repeated several times, " I am *savasch*,"—that is, " savage."

At Rouse's point, at the northern extremity of the lake, I first, on a beautiful moonlight night, touched Canadian soil, and for the first time in my life I was treated by custom-house officers as honest passengers ought to be treated.

"Gentlemen, have you anything that pays duty?"

We answered in unison, "No," and were then passed with bag and baggage, without the officers making any examination to discover whether we were or were not liars and cheats. On the quay was a post with a board, on which was inscribed, "No smoking allowed west of this board;" and I have often had occasion to notice how completely this wandering people must have the compass by heart to profit by such directions. Even in the labyrinth of streets in a great city they seem never at a loss, and on the addresses of letters you will see, "Two doors east or north of such a street."

Though in a railway train and at night, I immediately perceived indications of being in a different country. There were differences in the arrangements of the carriages, different figures and costumes, and from time to time I heard French, or rather Canadian, spoken. The mountains and hills of Vermont and New York had now entirely disappeared, and the moon shone over a wide plain, in which we could distinguish tracts of forest, of stony heath, or grass-land, intermingled with cornfields and thinly scattered villages. At some of these we stopped, and I could see that the outlines of the houses differed widely from those of the United States;—girls with their hands stuck in the pockets of their aprons, and young peasants with long nightcaps were talking to them as they lounged against the wall. We were passing through the counties of Acadie and Chambly, and at the last station, St Lambert, we came in sight of the mighty St Lawrence, its broad flood gleaming in the moonlight; the steam ferry-boat took us up as the steam carriage set us down, and we were soon again afloat. In former days, when steam did not toss people this way head over heels from one place to another, we should have passed the night in St Lambert, and have had time the next day before the "*bôteau*"* came, to have duly considered the situation, and made many philosophical reflections upon it; but there is now only time for this in winter, when the river is covered with ice, and the two shores are long separated from one another. We proceeded in a straight line across the river, but we had nevertheless several miles to go before we saw anything of the handsome "Silver Town." At last something glimmered silvery through the mist, namely the tin-covered houses and churches of Montreal. This

* Canadian for *bateau*.

metal, *un-precious* as it is, nevertheless preserves its white brightness a long time without rusting, and when the moon or the setting sun plays on the roofs and cupolas they produce an effect that Canaletto, or Quaglio, or any other painter of cities and houses, would be enchanted with. When I saw Montreal by common day-light, indeed, I could not help thinking the epithet of " Silver Town " far too complimentary; but, subsequently, when I saw the church towers under the rosy light of evening, they seemed to glow with internal fire, and I became of a different opinion.

The Americans regard Montreal and Quebec much as we do Memphis or Thebes, as places of the highest antiquity, and go thither if they desire to see something very old-world and European. The carriages in which we and our effects were received, on our arrival at Montreal, were certainly adapted to support this view. One cannot imagine how a coach-builder could hit on such a contrivance, and still less how such an old-fashioned, inconvenient machine could have continued in use to the present day. Fancy a large, high, clumsily-made sort of post-chaise, or rather box, hung between two rickety wheels. At the top of the machine sits the driver, and as soon as you have engaged him he backs it so as to enable you to step in at the door behind, and then away it jolts, you and your trunks and hat-boxes and carpet-bags tumbling about together, and settling your respective places as you can. For the use of this contrivance, too, you have to pay very dearly, at least if you get an impudent, extortionate Irishman to drive you, instead of a modest, good-tempered, honest Canadian.

In certain departments of social life,—hotels, railroads, river-steamers, and newspapers,—Canada is a good deal Americanized, and the great hotel at which we alighted, "Donnaganna's,"* was quite on the plan of those of the United States; it was, too, very republican in its spirit, according to which, while the great mass of the guests are admirably served, each individual appears neglected. When the multitude, summoned by the loud tones of the gong, comes crowding into the vast dining-room, they find a whole army of waiters ready to do their bidding, and supply every possible want; but if as an individual he requires out of the regular time as much as a cup of broth, he may starve before he gets it. Society at large finds saloons fitted up with princely splendour, but when you withdraw your individuality into your private room, you find

* Donnacona was the name of the first Indian Chief met with by Cartier, at his discovery of the St Lawrence, in the neighbourhood of the present Montreal. Probably the French Canadian family of Donnaganna derives its name from him.

yourself shut up in a mere cell, with four white walls, with a gas-pipe sticking out from the wall, at which you must yourself kindle a light, and where you may ring and stamp and call yourself hoarse even for a glass of water, and probably at last find that the only way to get it is to fetch it yourself.

CHAPTER IX.

MONTREAL.

MONTREAL is certainly the largest and most thriving town in America, northward of New York and Boston. In trade, wealth, and population, it is in advance of all other towns of Canada, and it has become the chief mart and metropolis of the life of the St Lawrence. With its 80,000 inhabitants, it may be considered a great city, and this number will, before long, be immensely increased. The advantages of its geographical position are such as to insure its advance.

The circumstance that immediately above the city the St Lawrence ceases to be navigable, and is interrupted by many rocks and rapids, doubtless gave occasion to the earliest settlement, as it was the furthest point to which Cartier, the discoverer, proceeded unhindered. He found, too, near the cataracts, an Indian settlement called Hochelaga, which must have been a sort of capital, as its name was so long current, and was even sometimes used to designate the whole country. After Cartier French ships often came so far, and the place was already well known, when M. de Maisonneuve in 1641 planted here the little pallisaded town, "Ville Marie," which was the germ of the present great city of Montreal.

The large island where this seed was sown is formed by the vast arms of the St Lawrence and Ottawa, and is on the whole a very flat and fertile country, certainly a rich Delta, formed by the deposits of the two rivers. It has on its eastern side a very striking natural object, a hill lying on the level ground like a large monument, which catches from afar the eye of any one who sails up the St Lawrence, and at whose foot Cartier and the founder of Montreal both probably landed. The fertility of this Montreal island (it is as large as a small German principality) tended of course to encourage settlement, and is still very advantageous for supplying the wants of a large town.

It is seldom that the sea-navigation of a river ceases only where its rocks and cataracts begin, but this is the case with Montreal. Ships of considerable burthen could sail right up to the town, but had there to be exchanged for Indian bark canoes. Marine animals, and even whales, sometimes come up the St Lawrence as far as Montreal, which therefore, though 400 miles from the sea, may be regarded as a sea-port.

The line of traffic along the cataracts and on the higher part of the river has now been improved by blasting rocks, and making canals and railroads; and the numerous countries and harbours of the interior, the towns and states on the great Canadian lakes, are thus placed in close connection with Montreal.

Another circumstance that contributed to the growth of Montreal was, that the Ottawa, the great tributary of the St Lawrence, mingles its waters with it at this point, and formed from the first a channel of communication with the west and north-west. It flows through a well-wooded and fertile country; brings down vast quantities of timber to Montreal, and takes from it the various products of civilisation. The woods are being rapidly cleared along its banks, land is being brought into cultivation, small towns are springing up, and steamers and railroads have made their way a hundred miles up its stream. It is often called in the country " Montreal's backbone."

The third line leading to Montreal is that of

Lake Champlain and the Hudson, by which we reached it, and this line has been now completed by railroads and canals.

Montreal appears, therefore, as the meeting-point and centre of four great natural high roads tending to various directions—that from the ocean of the north-east by the great stream of the St Lawrence,—of the upper river and the lakes,—of the river Ottawa,—and of Lake Champlain, which is the main link between Lower Canada and the United States. When, favoured so far by Nature, social life has thus been fairly kindled and burns so strongly at one point, capital and enterprise will soon open a way in other directions, which at first could not so powerfully influence it, and this has been recently exemplified in the line of railroad constructed between Montreal and the American town of Portland on the sea.

The geographical position and the importance of this line, and its organic connection with Montreal, will be easily understood if we consider first that the St Lawrence turns northward from Montreal, and reaches the ocean, from which at that city it is not far distant, by a great circuit. In those cold regions to which it flows it is often for a long time covered with ice and closed to navigation; and it is also at its mouth surrounded by great peninsulas and islands. Nova Scotia, Newfoundland, New Brunswick, Labrador, surround and block up its entrance, and cold habitual fogs, and frequent changes of wind, make the navigation among these islands slow and perilous. The free open ocean is not reached without a passage of nearly a thousand miles. The open ocean is practically much nearer to the Upper St Lawrence, namely, on the long sea-board of the American State of Maine. This coast, however, runs, like the St Lawrence, from south-west to north-east, leaving between it and the river an isthmus of about 200 miles broad.

The crossing of this isthmus, either by passengers or goods, was, of course, before the railway time a more difficult and expensive undertaking than the longer water passage by the St Lawrence; but the railroads have removed these difficulties, and made it possible to cut off that inconvenient country about its mouth, and connect Montreal, the centre of the commercial life of that country, more closely and intimately with the ocean. The fine harbour of Portland in the State of Maine has been found to be the point most easily reached, and the so-called "Grand Trunk Railroad" has been constructed between that port and Montreal. This remarkable railway will, however, only be completed when it shall have been found possible to bridge over the mighty St Lawrence.* Then only will it have become the actual artery of the Upper St Lawrence traffic. Vessels which find themselves on the banks of Newfoundland can then reach the end of the line at Portland by a much shorter, safer, and more convenient route than even Quebec—the port nearest the mouth of the St Lawrence—and this at all seasons of the year, even in winter when Quebec is inaccessible. For timber and other bulky and heavy goods the river by Quebec will remain the chief road, but all kinds of lighter goods will go by Portland, and the post will also naturally take this direction. Letters and information, often as important for transmission as goods, will, with the assistance of the telegraph line, be forwarded to Montreal with the utmost possible rapidity.

The whole line of coast, and the ports between Quebec on the north, and New York on the south, inclusive of these two cities, as well as Boston, Portsmouth, &c., may be regarded as the natural vents and outlets for the whole great system of the St Lawrence and the lakes, through which the connection is to be maintained between those fertile regions and the countries beyond the Atlantic.

* Victoria Bridge was opened by the Prince of Wales, in the present year, 1860.—TR.

Quebec maintained a connection with those regions from the earliest times by its river; and New York and Boston have long since established a communication by canals and railroads. Their youngest rival, Portland, with its recently-constructed road to Montreal, will probably in time become the most important of all,—for this reason, among others, that it occupies exactly the central point between the two extremes of Quebec and New York. The "Grand Trunk Railroad" seems to have had a prophetic inspiration in adopting this name. It is proposed, too, to carry this most direct line from the sea still further westward through the whole system of lakes. Lake Superior, it is supposed, will soon be reached, and many Canadian Britons prolong the line in thought as far as the Pacific Ocean; they have even represented it on maps with this prolongation, and as they lay down Portland for its eastern termination, place its opposite extremity on the Strait of Fuca, in the neighbourhood of Vancouver's Island.

The commercial advantages with which Montreal has been thus endowed both by nature and art, have called forth a vigorous life in the city at which the traveller is really astonished. At every step you find a building or an institution just begun or just completed; and not only in the streets, but far and wide over the country round, you might think yourself in a newly-founded city, rather than in one of 200 years old. The colossal Montreal of the future is now in the period of its infancy, and the small old Montreal of the present and the past, is opening wide its arms and making all possible room for the reception of its great progeny. Everything new is constructed on a scale that far exceeds present wants, and every effort is made to enlarge and extend what is old. In the long narrow old French main street for instance, the Rue Notre Dame, the new houses are being placed many yards further back on either side, so as to make a regular broadway like that of New York; and at the same time another main street of the grandest proportions, such as may become the capital of the St Lawrence, is in course of construction. This is the broad handsome St James's Street, which now wants only some additional length, and will soon stretch itself out like a pine tree. The public buildings, the bank, the post-office, &c., that already adorn this street, cannot readily be equalled for taste and solidity, and the new court-house is like a Greek temple, only larger and more massive than ever Greek temple was. The ground where 30 years ago snipes and partridges were shot in bush and swamp, is now covered with comfortable dwellings and churches of various denominations. Even the old French Catholics, who were formerly content with little dark chapels, having now under British rule attained to greater opulence and been kindled by British enterprise, have built themselves a new and stately cathedral capable of containing 10,000 persons. A new spirit seems to have been breathed into these long stagnant Canadian-French, and the great majority of them have frankly associated themselves with their English fellow-subjects, have cordially joined in all their speculations and industrial undertakings, contribute zealously to industrial exhibitions, and take an active part in committees and companies. The vast and solid quays of freestone which have been carried along the bank of the river are grand and useful public works, for the like of which London itself sighs in vain. Three millions of pounds sterling have passed for these improvements into the hands of architects, engineers, labourers, builders, and speculators, who are continually bringing some beautiful and useful work to a conclusion, and two millions' worth of stone is to be thrown into the great river to make a bridge that will not have its equal in the world, a fetter wherewith to bind the wildest and most gigantic of river gods. With another million the Canadians are hollowing out a terrace of the Montreal hill above the town for the basin of a magnificent reservoir, to receive the water brought from the Ottawa for the supply of the whole city. I witnessed some of the remarkable blasting operations for this basin, and I certainly never saw any work of the kind carried on on so grand a scale.

Holes of from fifteen to twenty feet deep and five or six inches in diameter were bored in the rock with a chisel worked by a horse, and filled with 110 pounds of gunpowder, and every blast rent away a piece of a rock as large as a house.

The great Market Hall of Montreal is another of the marvels exhibited to strangers as not having its equal in America; but there are certainly a good many things which have not their like in the whole American continent.

According to the custom of London and New York, and generally of all Anglo-Saxon cities, labour and pleasure occupy different quarters here. Business is carried on near the river, and the handsome half-rural residences of the merchants are in the suburbs. The business quarter contains only warehouses and country-houses, with the addition, recently, of some large manufactories, for the city possesses in the St Lawrence Falls an admirable water-power, which is now applied to machinery, and which I forgot to mention amongst the geographical advantages of Montreal. The suburban villas encircle the whole town, extending to the foot of the mountain, where they have often very lovely positions. The kernel of all these fine and spacious new buildings is, however, formed by the old French town, with its narrow streets, which cannot be entirely remodelled, and its little old-fashioned houses, very like those in our smaller continental towns; and some suburbs consist entirely of old wooden houses and sheds built close to and almost one upon the other, which seem expressly arranged to be burnt down altogether in the first fire.

CHAPTER X.

THE "ROYAL MOUNTAIN."

The long and finely-wooded hill, which is, as I have said, the only elevation to be seen for far and wide upon the flat island between the Ottawa and the St Lawrence, was called by Cartier the "Royal Mountain" long before a town existed here, and the first little settlement was called "Ville Marie," a name which is still retained for the Episcopal See. Gradually, however, the name of the hill was transferred to the town. Why the Spanish termination "*real*" should have been adopted instead of "Royal," I do not know, but some Canadians have informed me that that and not "royal" is the old form of the word in Normandy and Canada. The French peasants here corrupt the name still further and call it "Morreal." Since the name has been adopted for the town, the mountain has lost its royalty, and is called not "Montreal," but simply the mountain, and the city has already began to include it within her territory. The villas and the reservoir already touch its foot and its lowest spurs in the plain, and about half-way up there is a broad platform, or natural terrace, passing a considerable way round it, which it is proposed to make into a public walk, and it will certainly be one of the finest in the world. Another part has been taken possession of for the dead, and an extensive churchyard laid out, where the monuments are grouped in the most picturesque manner, though they are at present far less numerous than the trees.

We fairly lost ourselves in wandering about the terrace, where there are many cottages and small farm-houses, and from which there are magnificent views. You look first over the fertile island of Montreal, and beyond it, to the south, on the mighty St Lawrence, bounded to the east by a long range of mountains. All the features of a Canadian landscape, the rivers, the forests, the mountains, are bounded by such far-stretching lines, that the whole horizon appeared to be more extensive than I had ever seen it elsewhere. But the most attractive part of the landscape was the Ottawa river, winding away to the north, through massive forests, and the Lake of the Two Mountains, of which I could just obtain a glimpse. One has scarcely got into a country before what has been once seen begins to appear old, and the restless soul turns again with longing to the distant and the unknown.

We descended the mountain on its north-western side, which is probably much exposed to snow-storms, as the little French village lying there at its foot is called the *Côte de Neige*, its principal chapel, *Chapelle de Notre Dame de Neige*, and its chief hotel, *Hotel de Neige*. This was the first French, or rather Canadian, village I had seen. The people never call themselves French, and seem desirous of being regarded as aborigines of the St Lawrence. A stranger is often inclined to say, "You are a Frenchman, Sir, are you not?" and will then receive for answer, "Monsieur, je suis Canadien;" and throughout America, a "Canadian" means a person of French descent in the colony. Their English fellow-subjects are called "British Canadians."

The French Canadians have almost taken the place of the Indians, from whom they have derived many traditions and customs, and they speak of themselves as the original inhabitants. They are mostly regarded by us as horribly stupid, idle, and superstitious people—several centuries behind the rest of the world—a dead weight upon the march of progress, a black spot on the splendour of intelligence by which they are surrounded. The traveller is therefore agreeably surprised when he enters one of those "seats of darkness," a Canadian village.

It was Sunday when we descended into the Côte de Neige. The road was enlivened by gay promenaders, and pretty little one-horse chaises, in which some inhabitants of the village were returning from visits that they had been paying to relations and friends—for in their celebration of the day the French Canadians take the continental view, and consider that it was given for recreation as well as for prayer. In the pretty quiet cottages, and before the doors, we saw groups of the villagers engaged in friendly talk, and we ventured to enter one of the most humble looking, and were immediately understood and welcomed. The ancient mother, or grandmother, of the house set a chair for me by the fire, and turned to the other members of the family as if explaining, " *Eh bien, je comprend. Monsieur est voyageur, et il veut voir comme on vit en Conodó.*" The French of these good people would have been very agreeable if they would not have called *voir*, *savoir*, and *croire—vóar*, *savóar*, and *cróare*, &c. A broad *o* is constantly substituted for *a*—Canada is Conodo, *chats* are *chots*, and *les basses classes, les bosses closses*. This not very pleasing change proceeds, I understand, from Normandy, whence most of the Canadians are descended; and other peculiarities of the Canadian dialect are traced to that province and to Brittany and La Vendée, the difference being that here that dialect is spoken by all classes, and there only by the most uncultivated. Even well-educated Canadians are quite unconscious of the difference, and a pretty young Canadian lady once informed me, as of something quite comic, that the Parisians pretended the Canadians did not speak the purest French. She told me this in the most regular *Conodo* dialect, and then appealed to me as to whether she had the slightest provincial accent. She said she had once made a tour in France, and found that the peasantry spoke a much coarser and less intelligible dialect than any in Canada, and this I could confirm, but I really could not reconcile my conscience to telling her she had no provincial accent.

In most colonial countries it may be noticed that the language of the higher classes, when they do not keep up any communication with the refined society and the literature of the old country, tends to degenerate, while the peasantry, who lead a less narrow and stagnant life than in their original homes, lose something of their coarseness.

The present Canadian peasants are descended from soldiers, fur hunters, travellers, squatters, and all sorts of miscellaneous adventurers; and that such simple, honest, well-behaved people should be the offspring of such parents is a proof that human nature is just as prone, under certain circumstances, to improve and refine itself, as under others to grow degenerate and depraved.

As Romulus and his robbers became honourable Quirites, the progeny of voyageurs and scamps of various species has produced as primitive and innocent a people as Virgil could have desired for his Idyllic inspirations.

I found myself quite at my ease in this cottage. Besides the old woman who understood me so immediately, there was a man of middle age, a few boys, a very pleasing, neatly and even tastefully dressed young girl, and a bunch of little things of various sizes, but all clean and merry. You never forget for a moment the French descent of these people. Their features, their manners, their taste in dress, remind you continually of it. The lively, saucy boys, and the naïve and amiable little coquette of a girl, were genuinely French, and probably if we had had more time for observation we should have perceived the same or other traits of character, but all were considerably softened; the boys were not quite so saucy as the true *gamins*, the coquetry was not quite so gross; and all these qualities were mingled and blended in one tone of bonhommie and hospitality which is by no means characteristic of France. The cottage was in the most exquisite order, and its inhabitants were quite dazzling in the cleanliness of their snow-white linen. It was Sunday to be sure, but the every-day costumes that I afterwards saw did no discredit to the holiday one, in the *Côte de Neige*—and I could not help expressing to my old woman the pleasure their neatness gave me. "Vous êtes bien bon, Monsieur," she replied, "mais l'ordre et la propreté ce sont des qualités trés naturelles. Une famille malpropre! Ah Dieu préserve, une famille malpropre serait bien remarquée dans notre village. Et je croäi c'est le cas dans tous le Conodó!"

We were driven out of the cottage by the heat of the stove, the only thing in it that we did not find agreeable. The Canadians are noted in this country for the high temperature at which they keep their abodes. They have great Dutch-tile stoves, in which they keep up the fire the whole winter, and then enjoy themselves with heat and tobacco to such an extent, that when they come out in the spring they look quite pale, yellow, and withered. Now, in the autumn, their appearance was quite fresh and healthy.

CHAPTER XI.

CATHOLIC INSTITUTIONS.

THE Americans of the United States, now so numerous in Canada, who have founded so many various establishments in the towns, take, as merchants, contractors, engineers, road-makers, an active part in all its affairs. By the recent reciprocity treaty they have obtained the same rights of fishing and drying fish in the St Lawrence and on the Canadian coasts as the British inhabitants themselves; and besides these motives for visiting the country, the more opulent and idle classes of American citizens have begun to make a tour through the principal towns of Canada, its waterfalls and rivers, a fashionable excursion. Whole flocks of American tourists come from New York and more southerly places, by Lake Champlain, to the St

CATHOLIC INSTITUTIONS. 105

Lawrence, linger a few days in Montreal and Quebec, and then go up or down the river in the steamers.

To travellers of this class, the old Catholic institutions—the schools, hospitals, and convents—are generally objects of special curiosity; they are scarce in the Protestant South, and belong to the regular *stations*, at which an American tourist, obedient to his " Murray," is sure to stop. I confess I share this taste.

The old French convents and other public institutions of Montreal and Quebec have a remarkable history. A whole crowd of ecclesiastical orders in France used to look to Canada as to a field where an abundant harvest of Christian laurels was to be reaped. Jesuits, Franciscans, Dominicans, Brothers of Christian Doctrine and Sisters of Mercy, *Sœurs grises*, and *Filles de la Providence*—all sent out members of their societies, and scattered the seeds of their orders on the shores of the St Lawrence.

American historians sometimes speak of Canada as a military colony, whilst to the settlements of New England and Pennsylvania is ascribed a specially ecclesiastical and Christian character. In fact, the idea of a religious conquest—a *conquesta spiritual*, as the Spaniards say, was just as prominent as in any of the Spanish, English, or Portuguese establishments of America.

Sword and cross entered here into close partnership, and it would be hard to say whether the soldiers of the king, the agents of the trading companies, or the preachers and missionaries of the various orders, were most successful in discovering, conquering, and retaining the country. In the oldest maps, by the side of the representations of discoverers and *conquistadors*, we see those of monks and nuns. The wide field opened among so many heathen nations, and the possibility of a glorious martyrdom among the Indians, attracted so many champions of the faith, that at one time the Canadian towns had more monastic orders than the provincial towns of France itself; and of the 60,000 inhabitants which formed for a long time the whole population of the country, a very considerable part were shut up in convents. These old Catholic institutions of the French have just as little become extinct under the British rule as the Catholic Church itself; indeed, the Canadian Catholics existing at the time of the conquest, 1760, have increased under the protection of England to almost a million, and now, when all property has increased so much in value, the institutions formerly very poor have become wealthy and important. Their spirit, too, seems to be improved. In the Jesuits' time these frequent wranglings between Jesuits and Franciscans — between the regular and secular clergy—and the question, who was to stand at the head of the missions? often led to vexatious collisions. Every new order arriving from France, and for which spare lands and endowments had to be provided, awakened envy and uncharitableness. Now, under the English rule, these various societies live peacefully by the side of one another, and quietly occupy themselves with their schools, their sick, or their poor, according to the sphere of activity assigned them. A visit that I paid to these remarkable institutions, in company with a friend extremely well informed on all Canadian affairs, interested me much. My friend, who was of an old Canadian family, and had at one time been Mayor of Montreal, was the author of several elaborate treatises on some subjects connected with the history of the province, and had just concluded a remarkable work on the monastic orders of the city. He had even had drawings made for it by skilful artists of the costumes of the monks, nuns, and secular clergy; but the world will not profit by it, as it is in MS. and only intended as a present to a distinguished person, to whom it has been presented.

Our first visit was to the suffragan Bishop of

Montreal, in whom we found a handsome, agreeable, cultivated man, who conversed with cosmopolitan freedom on the affairs of the world at large. There was nothing provincial or Canadian about him, unless indeed that the clergy assembled round the stove in his anti-chamber, were smoking hard out of short clay pipes, like so many Canadian peasants. I hardly thought that the passion for smoking amongst the Canadians, which the English had often mentioned to me, would be allowed to display itself in these quarters; but there were these reverend gentlemen blowing clouds, knocking out the ashes, cleaning, and re-filling their pipes without being at all disturbed by the presence of their venerable superior. It may perhaps be partly explained from the circumstance that the missionaries on their journeys have frequent occasions to smoke the pipe of peace with the Indians, and may so have acquired the habit so inveterately that they cannot lay it aside even in their convents and episcopal palaces.

From the Bishop we drove to the Jesuits', who occupy a long new building called St Mary's School, and are employed more in the education of the young than in missions among the Indians or to distant countries. Protestant societies and the members of other orders do more now than the

Jesuits in a field where they formerly achieved so many wonders, of which glorious time the St Mary's College is itself a monument. The learned Father Martin had the goodness to lay before me the original of a map celebrated among geographers—that of the Jesuit Father Marquette, which is the first ever made of the Upper and Lower Mississippi and the adjacent regions, of which Marquette was the discoverer. I had often heard of it, and was much pleased to get it into my hands.

The oldest nunnery in Montreal is the convent of the Hôtel Dieu, which dates from 1644—that is, three years after the foundation of the town. It is devoted to the care of the sick and infirm, to which, as well as to education, the *Filles de la Providence* devote their time.

They have rapidly and energetically extended their sphere of action, and afford an example of the influence on America of the Catholic Church of Canada, and its flourishing establishments of the Lower St Lawrence. Several of the *Filles de la Providence* have been sent on missions of education and charity to the United States, and even to Oregon and Chili, and undertakings of this kind produce an effect, not only in distant countries, but in the strengthening and elevation of the minds of those left behind.

Of course we found establishments of the *Sœurs de Charité*, and the equally self-devoted *Sœurs Grises;* and the same cheerfulness, the same bright activity in works of charity, the same fresh, blooming, joy-beaming faces that I have seen on sisters of charity all over the world, also met me here. One of them, a handsome young sister, dressed like a Parisian, who showed us through a range of class-rooms and sick wards, I shall never forget. She was so zealous that we should see everything quite exactly—all the departments of the *bôtiment*—the rooms for the aged and infirm—for the young children, *et ceteró, et ceteró*—that I became quite charmed with the coarse dialect in which so much piety and goodness were expressed.

Every one in Montreal is full of praises of the *Sœurs de Charité* and the other benevolent sisterhoods; their zeal, their devotion, their Christian courage before the fear of death, which has been signally tried on two occasions,—in the year 1830, when the cholera raged in Canada; and ten years afterwards, when a pestilential ship-fever broke out among the numerous British and Irish immigrants, and destroyed many hundreds, including many of the brave nuns; and the Catholic matrons of the city also deserve high honour for their zeal in things which are above the praises of a traveller.

Many of them associated themselves with the nuns in those perils, and in one of the convents there is one department filled entirely by these ladies, who spare a part of their time from other occupations to make clothes for children and the sick. These convents often maintain themselves entirely by their labour, or with the assistance and contributions of such friends as these. In one of these I was led through a series of under-ground rooms, mostly devoted to household purposes; the doors of the kitchen were opened, and afterwards those of the wash-house, where many hands were actively employed. At last one was opened that had neither lock nor bolt; it was dark, but I could just distinguish a row of crosses on the wall, and a few stone monuments. "*C'est notre cimetière, Monsieur*," said my guide. The wooden crosses were for the nuns, the monuments for some benefactresses of the institution. Certainly a peculiar effect must be produced on the inhabitants of the house by having the chambers of the dead thus included in the same suite as their work and bed-rooms.

Among the Catholic educational establishments under the charge of men, the one that struck me most was that of the *Frères des écoles chrétiennes*. This order, which is widely diffused through the Catholic world, has in Montreal an admirably arranged school building, in which no fewer than 1800 boys are instructed by the monks.

The school-rooms were unusually spacious and well arranged, and at the two lessons at which I was present (those of writing and drawing), the performances of the pupils, the very judicious selection of copies and examples, the perfect order and cleanliness, and the remarkable excellence of some of the arrangements, made me wish I could send the directors of some European schools I know of to Canada, to study that of the *Frères chrétiennes*. I must repeat, however, that I was personally present only at the two lessons above mentioned.

The establishment of the " brothers of the Christian Schools " is maintained by the wealthy "Séminaire de St Sulpice," which also supports several others solely from its own funds; besides a seminary or college, where several hundred young men are brought up, it has schools for the humbler middle-classes of children of both sexes. This institution dates from a very few years after the foundation of Montreal, being at first a branch of the *Sulpiciens* of Paris, and afterwards an independent society. They undertake the divine service in several churches of the city, and eleven other members of the body devote themselves to instruction in the college; some serve an Indian mission on

CATHOLIC INSTITUTIONS.

the Lake of the Two Mountains; and the poor, the sick, and the orphan are in many ways assisted.

I closed my instructive day with a visit in which I had a second and private motive. Like most Canadian travellers, I had heard since I crossed the frontier of much talk of two unaccountable beings, denominated in Canadian *Lozevan* and *Shanseran*, but what on earth they were, whether men or evil spirits, or what else, I could by no means make out, but I heard both English and French people express themselves with respect to them in a manner that showed they were considered very important. You cannot help wishing to make out a riddle that meets you at every turn, and as I knew that the Seminaire de St Sulpice is one of the greatest "*Seigneurs*" in Canada, I thought I might gain from it some information concerning these mysterious beings, and accordingly I applied to the treasurer of the institution, who was good enough to fill up the gap in my Canadian knowledge.

Lods et ventes and *Cens et rentes*, for this is the written form of the words that had puzzled me, are the two principal still existing old seignorial rights appertaining to the possession of the fiefs or *seigncuries* into which Canada was divided by the French. By the first is signified the fine that a lord is entitled to claim from a vassal who desires to sell the land he holds of him, and there was probably a two-fold motive for the imposition; first, the lord naturally wished to keep old and faithful vassals and their families as much as possible attached to the soil, and to prevent the property from too frequently changing owners; and, on the other hand, the lord doubtless did not like to lose so favourable an opportunity of filling his pockets.

The vassal who had just disposed of his fief for hard cash was worth taxing, and the *Lods et ventes* amount to no less than one-twelfth of the price of sale. The *Cens et rentes* consist of certain annual dues, and are very trifling; at first they were only two sous the acre, and they are not much more even now.

Besides these two rights, the Seigneur in Canada has the mill-privilege, that is, he alone has the right of building a mill, and all his vassals must, for a certain fixed rate, have their corn ground at it.

Formerly the Canadian Seigneur exercised also the rights of *haute, moyenne, et basse justice*, but these rights, which were at no time frequently exercised, have become entirely obsolete since the English conquest, and all the much-talked-of seignorial rights are now confined to the three I have mentioned. It is nevertheless curious to find feudal institutions which have long since become extinct in France and Germany still keeping their place on American soil, and under the ægis of the English constitution. It may be that their apparent unimportance has prevented any great opposition being offered to them, but people have lately become aware that claims of this sort, even when they do not involve any very burdensome service, may be an obstacle to progress and act prejudicially on the country. In 1854, accordingly, a proposal was made in the Canadian parliament for their abolition, and for sweeping away altogether the old Canadian seigneuries; but the majority of the classes immediately affected, namely, the vassals and peasants, showed so little desire for the change, that it was evident it could only be effected in the course of many years, and that the greatest opposition it would have to encounter would be from the vassals and not from the Seigneurs.

The Canadian peasants are no Yankees. If the latter were affected by any of these ancient feudal restraints, they would not lose a moment in getting rid of them, and they would be always ready to make a present sacrifice for the sake of the future. They would find it perfectly intolerable that the Seigneur and his old-fashioned corn mills should occupy and block up water-privileges that could be turned to such good account for saw mills, paper mills, and similar works; and they would not endure for a moment his meddling in the sale of their property, and taking a lion's share of the produce. Since they are continually improving their land and then turning it into money, the Seigneur might be coming in with his claim every four or five years, and in the course of fifty would have drawn a sum equal to its whole value.

With the French Canadians, however, the case is quite different; they are fond of making savings from their little income, but their plan is to put it by, dollar by dollar, in a box, and they would greatly object to paying out a large sum all at once, if they were promised ever so large a future profit.

As they trouble their heads very little with industrial speculations, they find little to object to in their Seigneur's old mills, they pay willingly enough a few pence for each sack of flour, and rejoice greatly that it is their lord, and not they, who are called on for the large occasional outlay for the repair of the works. They do not regard even *lods et ventes*, and *cens et rentes*, as such words of fear. Their rents have been settled according to an old estimate of the value of the land, and are exceedingly low; their farms have risen so much in worth that they can well bear the tax of a few shillings, and if they were to get rid of it all at once by a single payment they would think they were exchanging a slight, almost imperceptible, evil for a very serious one. As for the *lods et ventes*, the case is still clearer. "Our fathers and grandfathers," they say, "lived upon this land, and our children and grandchildren will remain quietly upon it when we are gone. Our good Seigneur will never come in with his demand for a twelfth of the price of sale. Why should we pay a large sum to avoid a misfortune that, as far as we see, will never happen?"

Notwithstanding these objections, however, and the additional difficulties about the sums to be agreed on, and the mode of payment,—for if it were to be made in one sum the peasant would be ruined, and if in small instalments, the Seigneur embarrassed,—the Canadian Parliament, influenced by the spirit of the time, has resolved on the abolition of these dues, and the only question is about the mode of effecting the purpose. I heard it said that Parliament would assist the peasants by a special grant, and that abolition courts and banks would have to be organized.

In the meanwhile, a long time must, at all events, elapse before this change can take place, and the peasants will go on in their old way for many years, before they find themselves being carried along by the stream of improvement, so that there is not merely an antiquarian, but a practical, interest in inquiring into these old relations.

The whole of Lower Canada does not lie, even to this extent, under the oppression of the old feudal system, but only the part which was cultivated and inhabited in the time of the French, though it is certainly the best and most fertile part, extending over the best land on the St Lawrence, between the frontier of Upper Canada and the sea, and over the lower sections on the Ottawa.

The interior of the country, however, both to the north and south, but especially the latter, belongs to the Crown or the Provincial Government; and a great company, called the British-American Land Company, owns vast tracts. Both the Crown and this Company are constantly selling land to immigrants and speculators in the same way as the Government of the United States, and a great part of the land has therefore found its way into private hands. New settlements have been made, and new manners and customs introduced all round the French holdings, by people amongst whom there is no question of feudal rights.

Most of the French seigneuries are still in the possession of the families endowed with them by the king of France. They live in what are called

Manoirs, or Manor-houses, often in the midst of their peasants, and seldom in anything like what we should regard as a château, but in a habitation little superior to that of the peasants themselves. Most of the seigneuries yield only a very modest income, but there are a few larger, and I heard of one that had been sold for 150,000 Louis d'ors. Many of the seigneuries are in the hands of convents or other corporations, and many, since the conquest, have passed to English families. I have been told, but I do not know whether truly, that the rule of these English Seigneurs—perhaps because it is more systematically carried out—is often felt as more oppressive than that of the old French.

I have read, too, in an historical work on Canada that, since the time of the English Government, the feudal rights have been exercised with much more severity than formerly, and that the old French Government was milder to the vassals, and oftener considered what was fair and reasonable, instead of merely what was law.

As I was somewhat curious on the subject of these feudal tenures, I was favoured at the Seminary of St Sulpice with a sight of a printed statement of the receipts and expenditure of this body, lately published at the desire of the provincial Government, and from this document I take the following particulars :—The seminary possesses three of the largest seigneuries in Canada. First, the finest of all, namely, the fertile island of Montreal, bestowed on it at the earliest period, secondly, the seigneurie of St Sulpice, and, thirdly, that of the "Lake of the Two Mountains," on the Ottawa. On the thickly-peopled island of Montreal, every village holds its land of the seminary, sometimes, however, not immediately, but of intermediate vassals. Besides these seigneuries the seminary possesses several farms and allodial estates, and a great number of houses from which it receives rent. The whole brings in a revenue of 11,000 Louis d'ors. The *lods et ventes* and the *cens et rentes* on the island of Montreal alone bring in from £1800 to £2000 a year, but the two sources were unfortunately not distinguished in this *memoir*, nor was it stated from what population this sum was derived. From the seigneurie of the "Lake of the Two Mountains" the lord's mills have brought in four or five hundred a year, but it is not stated how many mills there are. The expenditure for the building and service of these mills seems to amount on an average to £300. In years when very thorough repairs have had to be made, £500 has been expended on them, but in others not more than £50. Before the proposal for the public abolition of these seignorial rights had been made, there were frequent voluntary abolitions, and it appeared that the seminary had received for these commutations in the year 1840 only £700, but in 1849, £5196; but in order to avoid any mistake as to the desire for this abolition in these seigneuries, or in Canada in general, it must be remembered that the seminary holds as Seigneur a great part of the land in the suburbs of the city of Montreal, and that the desire to get rid of these sort of troublesome privileges is much greater in the towns than in the country. It must also be borne in mind that of the ten thousand a year enjoyed as revenue by the institution, by far the greater part is again expended in the costs of administration, in the repair of mills, churches, and other buildings, in the maintenance of colleges and schools, and in the support of the poor, of orphans, and of invalids, so that at the end of the year a very trifling balance remains. The members of the seminary, according to the statement now before me, live in community, and receive no salaries or emoluments, beyond their board, lodging, and clothing, and what may be otherwise indispensable, as, for instance, in sickness.

I strongly advise every traveller proceeding from Montreal down the St Lawrence, and seeing, necessarily, so many of these old French villages, to inquire as much as possible into the peculiar political conditions under which these people live. Even the little that I learned concerning it made my journey and my visits to their villages far more interesting and intelligible.

CHAPTER XII.

THE ST LAWRENCE.

In all Canada there are, in a certain sense, only two villages—that is, two lines of village houses—one along the northern, the other along the southern, shore of the great river. The whole French population, at least, is divided among these two rows of almost uninterrupted water-side houses. They are indeed supposed to be divided into various villages—each with its own church; but the division is scarcely perceptible, for where one ceases another begins. There are certainly few countries in the world where the entire organization, and all divisions and sub-divisions, are so intimately dependent on a water-channel as French Canada. The three great political districts or governments into which the whole is divided—Quebec, Montreal, and the Trois Rivières, each of them as large as the kingdom of Prussia—have their central portions on both sides of the river, and extend their wings, south-east and north-west, into the wilderness, and their lines of demarcation are drawn perpendicularly to the river, and therefore run south-east and north-west, as do also the boundaries of the subordinate divisions, the districts and counties.

Nay, the seigneuries, and even the little farms, are rooted in the low fruitful land on the river-bank, and then cut their way south-east and north-west into the rocks and woods—which begin at no great distance from the stream. Still further; since these farms are held according to the French custom which prevailed among the colonists of Canada, the land has to be divided equally among all the children; the farms are again cut up into a number of still narrower strips—all divided on the same principle as the great political districts. All the fields present a front to the river; every child must have a bit of the bank, a little marsh, a little quarry, a little bit of forest and meadow; and the Canadians have carried this principle so far, that the strips of land look at a distance like the boards of a floor. The river appears to rule the whole country, like a long magnet amidst a mass of needles, all attaching themselves to it by their heads.

Considering French Canada apart from the rest, one may say that it consists of two strips of cultivated land; one north the other south of the St Lawrence, and extending from Montreal to the sea. Each of these is six or seven hundred miles long, and only a few miles broad; and the mildest climate, as well as the most fertile soil, is found along the river bank; a few miles inland it is much colder, and more inclement. The river runs straight on its course, does not divide itself into arms, and its tributaries, excepting perhaps the Ottawa, cannot bear the most distant comparison with it, in relation either to the volume of water or the advantages they offer for commerce. On the Ottawa merchant ships could, at the first settlement of the country, pass up as far as the inhabited country extended, and ships of war afford protection to its shores, and the first colonists naturally clung to the river which afforded them in case of necessity such a refuge from the Indians; so that it is easy to see how the country came to be laid out as it is. In the rear of the French, who had established themselves along the river, have come recently a second line of colonists, Scotch, Irish, and American, who have taken possession of the lands before unoccupied, and founded a few scattered villages; but the settlement of the country has proceeded most rapidly to the south of the river, where the climate is milder, and where Canada borders on the active states of the Union, which has sent forth her superfluous population and her enterprising pioneers, who have founded industrious little towns. But even this class of the population has been unwilling to go far from the river, as in Upper Canada from the Lakes which form its continuation; and they are seldom found further than fifty or sixty miles from its shores.

The inhabited portion of this northern half of Canada may therefore be considered to extend only to that breadth, but to eleven hundred miles in length, along the whole water-line from the western point of Lake Erie to the sea; although the Ottawa crosses this line, and there the settlements stretch out to the neighbourhood of Labrador, but they are much closer in the south-westerly direction.

I passed down the great river from Montreal by the night-steamer (as on the Hudson there were now no longer any day-boats); but as we had but a few hours' light, I could now see little more of the peculiar character of its shores than could be perceived by the faint moonbeams, which, when we neared the land, shone on small rows of houses belonging to those far-stretching river-villages, on the mouth of the river Richelieu, by which I had entered the St Lawrence, and on the tops of the towers of some old French churches at a distance. It marked out with uncertain lines of light the dark hulls of large ships that were moving past us on the broad river, and at last glittered on the wide surface of St Peter's Lake, the last of the numerous lakes of the St Lawrence, which spreads itself out about mid-way between Quebec and Montreal, and which we were now crossing diagonally, in the bright moonlight night. The traces of the ocean tide are lost in this wide basin—four hundred miles from the river's mouth; without the lake they probably would be felt as far as Montreal. The tide and the river seem to be here in conflict with one another, and it is perhaps from this cause that the St Peter's is the shallowest of all the lakes of the St Lawrence. The latter does not bring down any very large deposit of mud or other matter; but what it does bring it is mostly compelled to leave here, and thus have probably arisen the sand-banks found at the bottom of the lake.

In recent times a remarkable work has been nearly completed in the lake—a deep channel has been hollowed out in it along its whole length by means of steam dredges, so as to enable ships of large size to pass through it, and in this work they have come to a bed of such compact and solid material, that there seems to be little fear of the side walls falling in again; or at all events they will subsist for some time without any further help from art. It appears probable also that there are in the broad St Lawrence many natural channels which have not yet been discovered, at least the captain of a ship mentioned to me one, very fine and deep, that had been, until lately, entirely unknown. Should this be thought improbable in the case of a river so much navigated as the St Lawrence, it may be remembered that the same thing took place a few years ago in the case of one far more frequently traversed, namely, at the mouth of the Hudson, near New York. A channel of great depth and of the greatest utility to the navigation, hitherto quite unknown, was discovered in the labyrinth of parallel canals of which the bed of the river consists.

Though I could, as I have said, see during that night-passage but little of Canada outside the vessel, I could learn a good deal of it on board. We had as passengers a number of members of the Quebec parliament, at that time sitting, ladies and gentlemen from the counties on the neighbouring shores, French priests and landowners, and government officers, who altogether formed a very agreeable and instructive society. There were also members of parliament from Upper as well as Lower Canada, of both French and British origin, and the two nationalities seemed to harmonize as well here on the St Lawrence, as they had done just before on the Black Sea, and this was the more pleasing as there is not perhaps another river in the world on which they have shed each other's blood more frequently in mortal conflict. In the century preceding the final conquest of Canada there were at least a dozen English warlike expeditions sent to the mouth of the St Lawrence.

When the English at last got possession of the country, they found a population of only 60,000, and those living in great poverty. At first it appeared as if it were intended that these new subjects should be exterminated, as the French had been in Nova Scotia, and since also, very shortly after this conquest, the American revolution broke out, and France, in revenge for the loss of Canada, eagerly took part with the Americans, the position of the French subjects of England did not seem likely to improve speedily. They rose in revolt, with the assistance of the Americans, and after the latter had been driven from Canada, the country remained for many years under a military reign of terror, and even when this ceased (in 1784) an English party was formed, and continued to the end of the century, whose object was the entire and forcible Anglicising of the French inhabitants, and the uprooting of their language; but notwithstanding this their numbers increased during the industrial and commercial development of the resources of the country made under the protection of England. They seem to have multiplied like the children of Israel, since for the original 60,000 we now find nearly a million.

The notion of rooting them out, or even forcibly Anglicising them, was indeed given up at the beginning of the present century, but a great number of restrictive regulations were left for thirty years longer. "We were treated politically as children, sir," said a French Canadian to me, "and till 1837 were kept in a kind of slavish condition. Then we rebelled, and after that there followed what we call our Canadian revolution, for since then affairs have taken quite a different turn. The restrictions I allude to often affected the British colonists, as well as ourselves, and consequently in the revolt of 1837 and 1838, many of them took part with us, and *Quoique nous étions battus, ça nous a fait du bien.*

"The victorious British government, whose troops had beaten us, by no means laid heavier fetters upon us, as it mostly happens in such cases, but it allowed its eyes to be opened, and did us justice.

Many evils of which we complained were acknowledged and remedied. In the first place, the French colonists were by degrees raised to the level of the English; they obtained the same political rights, and the government took care more and more that, in the appointments to public offices, no regard should be had to nationality; many of the first and highest offices of the country are now filled by French Canadians. The population at large also was now admitted to a much higher degree of liberty and self-government.

"Not only have our town corporations, our country communes and counties, the same kind of half-republican constitution as in England—they choose their local magistrates on extremely independent principles, and have their local legislation quite in their own hands. Our Provincial Legislature and Executive too has attained to a degree of independence such as scarcely any British, or indeed any colony in the world, has ever possessed. Our Governor-General, the organ of the British government in our country, is as limited in his authority, as the Queen is in England. He has his responsible ministers at his side, whom he can certainly, according to law, choose as he pleases, but whom, in fact, he *must* choose as public opinion in the province requires. They are offered to him, and even forced upon him, just as Queen Victoria's Premier sometimes is; for if he should defy public opinion, and insist on taking his own favourites, he would find himself unable to carry on the government. They would not be admitted to parliament, where they should have a seat and a vote, and they would be unable to carry any measure, and be opposed in everything they undertook. One present excellent Governor-General has even accepted as ministers some of the leaders of the revolt of 1837, and men are sitting in our parliament, and even playing an important part there, who at that period had a price put on their heads, and would, had they been taken, have been put to death. Our ministry and our government, our Parliament and our legislation, are all modelled after those of England; but their independence and capacity for self-government has recently been manifested in the most satisfactory manner. On several occasions, when matters relating to Canada were brought before the British parliament, they declined to decide on them, and have referred to that of Canada, declaring that on the St Lawrence they were free to act as they thought best. All the money raised for the support of the government and the public expenditure here, is entirely under our own control; not a penny of it goes to England; it is laid out here for the benefit of the country itself, and an exact account rendered of every farthing. The connection with us is really rather an expense than a profit to England; and since the introduction of free trade, England does not enjoy any peculiar commercial privileges. The recent Reciprocity Treaty places even the Americans almost on a level with the English and with ourselves. England has no other benefit from us than our friendship and brotherly feeling towards her, and the circumstance that we keep open a desirable field for emigration for her.

"The result of all this is a wonderful reconciliation of all parties, including the French and British colonists, and an extremely favourable and friendly feeling between the young colony and the old country. There are no traces now of any leaning towards our great neighbour republic, now that while enjoying royal protection we have as many public and private rights as if we were republicans. Under these circumstances we, of course, desire the continuance of the connection with England—a connection from which we have no disadvantage whatever, but, on the contrary, many essential and important advantages. With respect to us French Canadians, the leaf has been completely turned. Whilst formerly Great Britain had in us a domestic enemy, always ready to conspire with foreigners against her, it now possesses in us the most important counterpoise of foreign influence; that is to say, against the possible longings of our republican neighbours. There exists indeed among our young men a small party whom we call ' *Rouges,*' who are extravagant admirers of republican institutions; but the mass of the French population is essentially conservative, and wishes, as far as possible, to maintain the *status quo*. I heard once of an American who, when he was travelling through our country, and observing the antiquated ways of our French peasants, observed that if they, the Americans, got the country into their hands, they would soon improve the old-fashioned French off the face of the earth—and this is just what our people dread—they think, and I believe rightly, that a union with the Republic would bring on the rapid decline of their language, their customs, and their nationality, which would melt away and disappear before those of the Americans, as formerly those of the aborigines of the country did before theirs. This fear keeps us French attached to old Europe, even though it is represented to us by Great Britain; and Great Britain on her side is doubtless influenced by it, and among other liberal proceedings allows the French clergy all desirable freedom."

"Have you old-fashioned French," said I, "drawn

closer to the English in social relations; for instance, do you take any part in their industrial speculations?"

"Ça commence, Monsieur, ça commence," was the reply. "On the whole, it cannot be denied that our old Canadian population, if not in moral character, does certainly stand far behind the English in knowledge and education. It is but lately that we have formed any of the literary societies which have existed so long amongst them; but we have now in the suburbs of Montreal and Quebec, lecture and reading-rooms for French young men as well as for English. Even the French merchants, though mostly only small dealers (for almost all the first houses in Montreal and Quebec are of British origin), have gradually adopted the more energetic and practical methods of their fellow-colonists. Most of the French houses have adopted the English as their language of business, not merely in their correspondence, but also in their counting-houses and private books, and this not only because it is more convenient in Canada, but because they consider it generally preferable for commercial purposes. The well-educated French here write and read English as well as their own language, though there are certainly many remote Canadian villages where my good countrymen neither read nor write that or any other language. *Mais ça commence aussi, Monsieur, ça commence.*"

The worthy Canadian M. P. who made me these and other communications, was here called away; and a young Briton, who had been listening to our conversation as we talked, leaning over the bulwark on the deck of the steamer, now took his place, and as the Frenchman had touched last on a topic that specially interested him, that of the state of education amongst the lower class of the French, he began to inform me of his views on the subject.

"I can confirm," he said, "all that that gentleman said of the gross ignorance of our French rural population. I have lived long among them and like them very much; they are the most inoffensive people in the world, but in many parts of the country they are densely ignorant and superstitious, and that chiefly because they are wholly under the control of their priests. In all their doubts and perplexities they go to him and ask him what is to be done, and if he is content with anything, all is right. That they cannot read and write is very agreeable to the priests, for they read and write for them. When one of them gets a letter he goes straight to the priest with it, and he reads it, and answers it; or, if he cannot, he sends the peasant with it to the village notary, who always has an understanding with the priest, and both together settle everything as they think proper. If you only do not in any way interfere with their priests, you will find them the most peaceable and sociable people in the world, and it is really delightful to watch them in their daily quiet ways, and in their homes among their families. If you do not interfere with them they never will with you, there is only one nation that they cannot get on with, but that is the fault of the nation in question."

"Probably," said I, "you mean the newly-arrived Irish? It seems to me that no one in America agrees very well with them."

"Yes, sir," said the Briton (who was a Scotchman), "and in the American States the Irish disagree just as much with the Germans. Out here in Canada they come into competition with the people of the country in many little occupations, as petty dealers, as servants, or cab drivers, or in the hotels and steamers, and then there are conflicts between the two nationalities, which in Europe, on account of their common religion, their common origin (the Celtic), and their common Anti-British sympathies, so ostentatiously proclaim their friendship for each other."

I had myself heard Canadians express aversion to the Irish, especially on account of their quarrelsome ways and their tendency to fight on every occasion. It is sometimes thought indeed that the French-Canadians carry their peacefulness to excess. "I never fight," said one of them to the above-mentioned Scotchman, "I run away" (je me sauve). And yet it is these very French-Canadians who encounter so many dangers, and support so many hardships, throughout all north-western America, and who make the bold and indefatigable voyageurs.

CHAPTER XIII.

QUEBEC.

On board an American steamer it is necessary to lose no time in entering your name in the large book which lies open for the purpose in the chief cabin, and in placing beside it the number of the state-room you mean to occupy. If you do not attend to this you run the risk of being put off as I was with what no one else will have. The sleeping-rooms farthest from the engine are naturally the most sought after, but the one allotted to me was exactly between the engine and one of the paddle-wheels, so that I was between fire and water. The walls were merely board partitions, so that I heard on one side all the creaking, thumping, groaning, and squeaking of the machinery; and on the other, the rush of the perpetual cataract down the side of my cabin, in addition to every manœuvre of the stokers, every bang of an oven-door, every blow of the poker on the coals, and a temperature that seemed to me very little below that of the boiler itself. All which circumstances had this advantageous result, that I was one of the first upon deck on the following morning.

We were already in the neighbourhood of Quebec, and near the remarkable narrows above that city at Cape Rouge. It is here with the St Lawrence as with the Hudson at West Point, the river is hemmed in by heights, which it has probably broken through. These narrows may be regarded as the pointed extremity of the long, broad ravine filled by the lower St Lawrence. Near the island of Anticosti, at the mouth of the river, the ravine is thirty or forty miles wide. It is contained between two mountain-ranges that run to the south-west, and becomes continually narrower and narrower as it proceeds in that direction, till at Quebec and Cape Rouge it terminates with the ordinary dimensions of a river. Quebec* lies therefore at the end of the middle and the beginning of the lower St Lawrence. The tide, which in the Lake of St Peter's rises only two or three feet, has at Cape Rouge a rise of several fathoms, and in the spring

* The word Quebec is said to be derived from an Indian one, signifying "narrow part of a river."

an enormous mass of ice is formed here, which blocks up the river, and lies longer than in any other part of the St Lawrence. It seems likely that the river was once blocked up here by rocks and mountains, as it occasionally is now by ice, and that these mountains surrounded a great bay, which we now call the Lower St Lawrence. The Upper St Lawrence at that time flowed in a quite different direction, or it formed great inland seas without visible outlet, like the Caspian, until at last it broke through the barrier, and poured itself out probably in cataracts like that of Niagara. There are still cataracts enough near Cape Rouge, namely, that of the well-known river Chaudière coming from the south, and immediately below Quebec the Falls of Montmorency, and of the Rivière St Charles. It is the region of cataracts, such as are not seen again between here and Montreal.

The view was striking in the highest degree, the mighty river being hemmed in by long curved walls and masses of rock, with only a very narrow level strip of shore near the water's edge, and that strip covered by houses;—there are, as I said, houses all along the banks of the St Lawrence,—and you might imagine on seeing these endless lines that Canada was one of the most populous countries on the face of the earth. Of the three millions of inhabitants of Canada, at least 900,000 live on the banks of this river, and are likely enough to be seen by the traveller from the water, so that you are pretty sure not to feel lonely on the St Lawrence, but at Cape Rouge and Quebec it is more lively and busy than elsewhere. The whole St Lawrence round the rocky heights of Quebec, and several miles above it, as far as Cape Rouge, is one harbour, and on the rocky shore are several deep bays called Coves. These small bays, which are surrounded by rocks and forests, are filled by enormous stores of wood, and the rafts which come down from Ottawa and Montreal, as they are there protected from the effects of the tide and from the ice. The trade in timber forms the principal commerce of Quebec. Wood is a very bulky article, requiring many vessels to fetch it, and causing therefore much animation in the places where it is shipped, and Quebec is surrounded for miles with busy scenes of this kind. Even the little wood harbours in Norway look important with their massive wares and the bustle of getting them shipped, but there would be little interest for the spectator in such a spot if gold, or indigo, or silk, to the same value, were exported.

The common phrase of a "forest of ships" would not suit Quebec, and, indeed, a wood of long monotonous masts, like so many gigantic bean-stalks, would be neither picturesque nor poetical, but the harbour of Quebec, where the vessels lie scattered about in groups, is so in a high degree. Some lie in the middle of the river, others before one or other of the little coves; here and there is one anchored alone like an arctic explorer by the side of a rugged mass of rock. Just before the navigation closes for the season is the liveliest time, and Quebec has then nearly half as many inhabitants again as usual, namely, 100,000 instead of 60,000, in consequence of the flocking thither of wood-dealers of all kinds, sailors, and others. As the river below is adorned by ships and rocks, so is the lofty terrace above it by handsome villas, which appear among groves and woods, pleasantly looking down on the river below. Amongst them is the celebrated Spencer Wood, the residence of the Governor-General of Canada, Lord Elgin.

It was a brilliantly beautiful autumn morning when we came in sight of this attractive scene, and passed through it for several miles, until we anchored at the foot of the bold and lofty Cape Diamond (on whose declivities Quebec is built), and then made our way through the narrow and crooked streets of the lower town to the upper mountain terrace, and the hotel to which we were destined.

CHAPTER XIV.

CAPE DIAMOND.

I HAVE in vain searched through old maps, histories, and chronicles of Canada, in vain, as we Germans say, " broken my head " to find out who first bestowed on the remarkable rock that serves as the foundation of Quebec, the name of Cape Diamond. It may have been the founder of the city, the often-mentioned Champlain, or it may have been Cartier, who first navigated the St Lawrence, but whoever it was, the name is not without meaning. Standing on the extreme point of the promontory occupied by the renowned citadel, and looking round you, you will acknowledge that you have at your feet a real gem of the country—the Koh-i-noor of Canada, set *à jour* in grand ranges of mountains, far-stretching plains, and long bright streams, which issue from it like rays.

This diamond is cut on one side by the great St Lawrence, which washes its cliffs on the south, and, unfortunately, sometimes washes them off. In quite recent times, a whole wall of rock was loosened by it, and fell, burying houses, men, and ships in its ruin. On the east side, the setting is formed by the small river St Charles, which turns at a right angle from the St Lawrence, and has worked out a similarly steep and lofty wall from the rocks. It forms at its mouth a wide valley, or level, of more than eight miles broad, which is covered by houses and villages.

The rocky headland itself rises into a bold and lofty promontory of 300 feet high, and presents a most imposing appearance to any one approaching it from the sea; and Champlain must have been blinder than the old Byzantians, who overlooked the Golden Horn, if he had failed to notice this diamond of the country, or to perceive that it was the true site for the capital of New France. Here was a natural harbour, a natural fortress, and immediate connection between the ocean and the interior, and moreover an abundance of most fertile soil, concentrated into one focus. The question where the Europeans were to sow the seed of the capital of the St Lawrence must have been at once decided.

From the summit of the promontory you enjoy a prospect almost unequalled in its kind, and see below you the remarkable old town, with its houses covering two sides of the mountain, gathered here and there upon level masses of rock, adapted for markets or other public places, and connected with one another by crooked ascending streets. Sometimes the houses run in streets at various heights round the mountain, and sometimes drop down to the level of the river, and form narrow lines between it and the rocks. Finally, they climb up to the brow of the Cape, and there spread out to the very walls of the citadel.

The river, which has been considerably narrowed from Cape Rouge, opens out again widely after passing Cape Diamond, and forms, in sight of the town, two great arms which clasp the Isle of Orleans—like the Island of Montreal, one of the paradises of the St Lawrence. It is extremely fertile, well peopled, and adorned by several pretty, quiet villages. At the earliest period the French called it the Isle of Bacchus, because they found its woods full of wild grapes. To the right of Cape Diamond, opposite on the other side of the narrow, lies its twin-brother, Cape Point Lewis, also covered with houses, churches, and country houses, which together constitute a sort of suburb to the capital. It looks like Quebec reflected in a mirror, and beyond it appear long ranges of hills and mountains one above another, which form the boundary between Canada and the United States —the last summits being those which rise from the forest state of Maine.

To the left, instead of frowning rocks, lies a pleasant lowland covered with farms and villages —the mouth of the St Charles—and behind it again mountains, as in the south. There is a range of still wilder mountains which runs north-eastward along the St Lawrence, throwing out branches to Labrador, and south-west to Ottawa and the neighbourhood of Montreal. Farther west, branches of the same craggy range surround the basin of the Ottawa and the Upper Canadian lakes, and separate their waters from those flowing into Hudson's Bay. This remarkable system of mountains has as yet received no name from our geographers, unless we admit for such— "The Mountains North of the St Lawrence," or "The Mountains of Lower Canada;" but a Canadian historian has christened them the *Laurentides* —a very suitable appellation, for they accompany the river with fidelity and perseverance, and stand like watch-towers along its whole line. The name, therefore, has been quickly adopted by Canadian geographers and historians, and deserves to be generally introduced. Among English geologists the name of the St Lawrence has already been turned to account in this way, for they have called a certain extensive formation of sand and clay, " The Laurencian Deposit."

This deposit is a modern product of the ocean, and is filled with the remains of molluscs and other marine animals, of genera and species still living in the neighbouring seas. It fills, although much broken and interrupted, all the lower interior of the basin of the lower St Lawrence, surrounds Lake Ontario, and ends near the Falls of Niagara. The St Lawrence and its arteries are quite embedded in it, and the river is, therefore, the fittest sponsor for it, and no less for the above-mentioned mountains.

The many-peaked Laurentides, rising out of a sea of forest, mark out not only the boundaries of inhabited Canada, but also of the whole of cultivated America; beyond these bare and desolate summits is nothing to the " end of the world " but a measureless wilderness. Beyond the limits even of the Quebec panorama, whole provinces contain but a few scattered Indians; so that this panorama may be regarded as an oasis—an extremely animated, thickly peopled, and well-cultivated oasis—in a desert of primeval forest, rock, and sea. Thus far, and no further, does American civilization reach towards the north, and, like an expiring light, blazes up once more into a brilliant flame.

What struck me most in this view, as in that by Montreal, was the colossal proportion of every object—mountain, river, and plain, the vast extent seen at once from a comparatively so low point of view. You may climb with immense toil many an Alpine peak which rises far above the clouds, without being so much impressed with the elevating feeling that you have a vast portion of the creation at your feet as when you look from this Quebec diamond of only a few hundred feet in height, and it is not to be obtained only from the summit of the rock. You may get the same, with countless pleasing variations, from many points outside and inside the town; from "Durham Terrace," a superb platform, where the old French castle of St Louis formerly stood, and which is now being levelled, and laid out as one of the most beautiful public walks in the world. Another view is obtained from the ramparts, also an attractive promenade, seeming high in the air; or from the esplanade; and it surprises you from many public places and corners of the city, as well as when you drive along the heights, but perhaps best of all from the walls and bastions of the mighty citadel by which they are crowned.

This citadel of Quebec, which I took occasion to visit, is one of the greatest fortifications of the New World. It has been enlarged and improved down to the most recent period. When you contemplate these massive formidable walls of freestone, and wander through the elaborately and systematically complicated labyrinth they form, fancy them well manned by stout Englishmen, and notice the heavy cannon commanding every point of the mountain and valley of the St Lawrence, you feel induced to think very little of all the talk you hear about the indifference of England to her Canadian possessions, and her perfect willingness to leave the provinces to themselves, and allow them either to establish an independent state, or to join the American Republic, as they may think proper. On the contrary, you seem to see here a bit of the paws of the lion, which has his teeth and claws perfectly ready, and in case of need could give a good account of any one who offered to meddle with his property.

How and in what way the military recollections of Quebec might be renewed, is what one scarcely likes to inquire in the midst of so fair a peace as now shines over the country. There are enough of such recollections; but you cannot help seeing that, while the rock presents a threatening and almost impregnable front to the water, there lies a field where such laurels might be reaped, at the back of the head where the promontory stretches out into a wide level surface where alone an ascent of the position, an assault, and a battle would be practicable. These are the " Plains of Abraham," celebrated for more than one engagement, and which extend from the walls of the citadel, like the high fields before Prague, on which Frederick the Great and others fought the "Battles of the White Mountains." The city of Quebec has been indeed often enough shot at from the water, set on fire, and destroyed; but only once, as far as I know, was an attempt made to storm the rock itself and the whole position from the water, and then it was by a daring officer, who, knowing the insufficiency of the force at his disposal, was obliged to attempt some extraordinary exploit. This was General Montgomery, during the time of the American Revolution, when the troops of the new-born republic had revolutionized almost all Canada, and the country appeared just as much lost to England as the rest of her North American colonies.

In the year 1774 he found himself, with a small body of 1300 men, before Quebec—at that time almost the only spot remaining to the Royalists in all Canada. The fewness of his troops made it impossible for him to attempt a regular siege, or an attack on the strong fortifications and bastions towards the " Plains of Abraham," and he was induced to try something unexpected. He determined to surprise the fortress in the night, by climbing up the precipitous rocks, where an attack could be least expected; but his enterprise failed. The small bodies of men whom he had sent to different points for a feint were cut off or beaten back, after they had advanced a little way; but Montgomery himself, who led the main assault, met a speedy death. He had not advanced far upon a rocky path covered with ice and snow, when he suddenly discovered a masked and well-placed battery of the English, which immediately opened fire upon him, and stretched the greater part of the gallant little band, himself included, in their blood upon the snow. The death of Montgomery, who was as much esteemed for his humanity and moderation as for his energy and valour, put an end to the whole attempt upon Quebec, and was the beginning of a turn in the tide of affairs, by which the Americans finally lost all their positions in Canada.

No monument has been erected to the general, esteemed as he was by friend and foe, but the numerous visitors from the United States do not fail to point out the rocky path on which he was marching, the spot where he was shot down on the fatal night, and the hole whence his body and those of his adjutant were drawn out of the snow.

This case alone excepted, the struggles for the possession of Quebec have mostly taken place on the level ground to the rear of the fortress; for instance, that decisive battle between the French and English, under generals Montcalm and Wolfe, which resulted in the conquest of Quebec, and ultimately of all Canada, for the English. The configuration of the battle-field is not much altered to the present day, and the principal points of the memorable engagement of the 13th September, 1759, may still be recognized. We looked down on the little wooded river-bay, by which the British general, Wolfe, with the main body of his army, landed in the night between the 12th and 13th. It is one of those small coves that I have already described, and was at that time called by the French "*Anse du Foulon.*" It is now "Wolfe's Cove." The shores are here not quite so steep as at some other places, and whoever climbs them finds himself at once before the fortifications to the rear of the citadel. General Wolfe, who had long had his headquarters in the plains below Cape Diamond, where his ships were anchored, had, by a skilfully masked manœuvre, succeeded in surrounding the Cape and the whole peninsula of Quebec, and of throwing a part of his army in ships into the waters above the town. The French general commanding in the city and fortress believed this was only a small detached corps, and had his attention specially directed to the points below Quebec; but in reality Wolfe himself, with the main body of his army, had crept round the promontory, landed at the little wooded bay, ascended the heights, surprised the feeble French out-post, and suddenly appeared in full force on the "Plains of Abraham."

Besides that little bay, which can never be effaced by human hands, with its historical interest, we find on the field itself a lasting memorial of the conflict, in a natural hollow or trench, where the young commander when he had received his mortal wound was brought to die.

Montcalm, still under the idea that the attacking force could not be the main army of the English, had advanced from the citadel with half his troops, and thoughtlessly begun the battle, which soon turned in favour of his enemies, but which at the same time removed their chief for ever.

Wolfe was leading his grenadiers to a bayonet charge, when he received a shot in the breast and fell. The spot where it happened is not exactly known, but his friends carried him a little to the rear—to the above-mentioned hollow, and just as he was breathing his last, a voice near him exclaimed, "They fly!" With a last effort he asked, "Who?" The answer was, "The French!" and then the dying hero fell back smiling contentedly, and expired. The place is marked by a monument, and every one knows West's picture of the Death of Wolfe, which I have myself often seen; but here on the spot I discovered that the painter had drawn on his fancy, and not on his knowledge, for the scenery and background of his picture.

The whole spot, up to the walls of Quebec, offers much the same aspect that it must have done in the year 1759. It is a desolate, houseless, treeless spot, full of holes and inequalities, and here and there of the remains of the old French batteries.

"Probably it was near one of these," says the historian of Canada, Professor Garneau, " that the French leader Montcalm met his death, a few moments later than the fall of Wolfe. Like Wolfe, he had before been slightly wounded, and, like him, was shot in the body while fighting bravely, and thrown down under his horse; and his men, cursing the mischance, carried him from the field into the town. The fallen heroes, opposed to each other in mortal conflict during their lives, have been reconciled in death; for a common monument has been erected to them in the public garden at Quebec; and it is still more gratifying to find that the two nationalities, who carried on so long and bloody a conflict with one another, are now so completely in harmony that the French have subscribed as willingly to the monument to Wolfe as the English to that of Montcalm. The latter is easily intelligible, for Montcalm was a brave and esteemed man, though unfortunate as a general; and it is easy for the victorious to show generosity to the memory of a respected though vanquished foe; but that the Canadian French should have contributed to a monument to their conqueror Wolfe, and even regarded it as a duty to do so, this I saw explained in a Canadian Journal. "Wolfe," it is said, "did not by his victory so much bring the French under a foreign yoke as free them from an antiquated one, extremely unfavourable to progress. He and his Britons founded a new era for Canada, and the 60,000 poor colonists who have been raised by his means to a million of prosperous artizans have much to thank him for."

After leaving the "Plains of Abraham," I had a delightful excursion along the heights, past many most beautiful villas and country seats which lie on the elevated banks of the river, to the magnificent park of Spencer Wood, the residence of the Governor General. The villas belong to rich merchants, and the French would certainly never have established such comfortable and luxurious dwellings in the midst of the Canadian woods if the English had not shown them the way. The old French Manoirs, in which some of the Seigneurs still live, bear the same relation to them that the old-fashioned "*bâteaux*," still occasionally seen on the St Lawrence, do to the luxurious steamers of the Anglo-Saxons.

CHAPTER XV.

THE VILLAGE OF BEAUPORT AND THE FALLS OF MONTMORENCY.

FROM the heights of Quebec you can see again to the north-east part of that long row of houses which you have already observed above the city. This is the village of Beauport, which runs for miles along the shore parallel with the river.

We had engaged one of the little jolting, inconvenient Quebec *droshkies*, and were rumbling along over stock and stone through the principal streets of this village, to reach the Falls of Montmorency, which are about six miles off.

I never passed through a Canadian village without keeping my eyes wide open, that I might look through doors and windows at the pretty interiors, and watch the groups of peaceful inhabitants at work, or gossiping about their fires, or passing from house to house among their neighbours.

Here at Beauport they seemed now to be engaged in some important affair. A long procession of men and women in galá dress was moving on before us, and entering now this house, now that; and completely filling it. We alighted from our carriage and peeped anxiously through an open door, but one of the peasants seemed to disapprove of this, and said, "What do you want, gentlemen? What business have you here?"

As we were convinced that a Canadian peasant is never rude unless he thinks he has good cause, and that even then he is easily appeased, we did not allow ourselves to take offence, but said, "We are strangers, Sir; this is our first day in your country, and we are a little curious to see the people and the happy couple, for you are, doubtless, celebrating a wedding."

"Ah c'est ça! Très bien, Messieurs; descendez, descendez toujours, et entrez: Soyez les bienvenus. Oui, sans doute ce sont des noces."

We accepted the invitation, and looked in at the cheerful assembly, and I think I never saw so many handsome, well-dressed, well-behaved people at a peasant's wedding. There were healthy and well-made young men, good-tempered old men and matrons, lively blooming girls, and, in the midst, the be-garlanded and happy, but mute and embarrassed, bridal pair. Pictures and novels tell us often in England of the " good old times," but here in Canada you may see them in living reality before you, not in ink or on canvas, but in flesh and blood.

" This is only a little visit, sir, that our young pair are making to their friends," said the man whom I had first addressed; "they are going through the whole village to one relation and neighbour after another. This is the season for weddings among us. At the beginning of October every one gets married who is not married already, that he may get settled, warm, and comfortable for the winter. We had to-day in our village four weddings, four bridal pairs going about to pay their visits."

Wherever a wedding is going on, nobody has eyes and ears for anything else, and the whole body of villagers accordingly went flocking after these, like a swarm of bees after their queen; and though we would gladly have heard something more of Canadian wedding customs, it was quite impossible to obtain the services of a cicerone who might have instructed us in them. Since we had alighted, however, we loitered a little to look about us, and, in order to make our experience as varied as possible, we entered first a very humble and afterwards an opulent dwelling.

We found the cottage small but very neat and clean, the windows adorned with flowers, and a pretty little flower-garden outside. This love of flowers is almost universal amongst the French settlers, but much less so amongst those of British origin. Some little coloured prints of Catholic saints hung on the walls, and some large shells lay as ornaments on the press. It seemed to me as if I were entering a cottage at Ostend or Boulogne, I had never seen in America anything in such old European style. Three plump, almost too plump, women—mother, daughter, and daughter-in-law— were seated round a large rough wooden table with two female neighbours, and all industriously at work, making a holiday gown for one of the party. Some nice healthy-looking children were also engaged in stuffing something with large needles. The company were all very friendly and polite, and did not appear in the least disturbed by our visit. We told them we intended to visit also one of their neighbours, named Bienville. " *Ah v'là Monsieur Bienville ! Oh oui, Messieurs, là vous verrez quelque chose—chez nous ça ne vaut pas la peine. Nous n'avons que de petits emplacemens. Mais Monsieur Bienville c'est un gros habitant! un des plus gros messieurs dans le village!"*

The word *paysan* appears to be scarcely ever used here. *Habitant* has quite taken its place, and has spread over the whole of what was formerly French America. In Louisiana, and on the lower Mississippi, the French colonists are also called *habitant,* and their settlements *habitations.*

We found the *gros habitant* busy at a lime-kiln situate on the side of his house near the river, and we noticed these lime-kilns scattered about everywhere among the houses of the district. Monsieur Bienville brushed the lime-dust from his clothes as soon as he learned our wishes, and accompanied us to his abode, where we found everything very nice, neat, and pleasant. We were introduced to the madame and mademoiselles *habitantes,* charming French women, who, by their simple, unpretending, and amiable manners, made a very favourable impression on us. They entertained us with milk and excellent snow-white bread, which had been "blessed by the priest," and was specially intended to be given to strangers. During the conversation we certainly perceived that these people were deficient in knowledge and education, but not in natural intelligence or good will. Their rooms were very spacious; to an American they would have appeared old-fashioned in their furniture; but they had a much gayer and more original effect than those of Yankee settlers. On the wall hung several pictures, and amongst them one of Napoleon, who, although they never fought under him, is almost as popular with the Canadians as amongst the peasantry in France. There was also a "Sentence for the month of October," in a gilt frame, and at the side of it an "*Application* or *Pratique*," and my hosts informed me that they received one of each of these from their priest every month. The "Sentence" was a well-chosen text from the Bible, and the exposition showed the mode of its application to peasant-life in Canada. Some people may be inclined to see in these sentences another proof of meddling priestcraft; but do they think that if the priest did not give the sentence the peasant would choose it for himself, or would he esteem it so highly if he did?

Our host was a temperance man, and had renounced every sort of alcoholic drink, and he pointed out to us a "Temperance Column," which stood on an elevated spot in the village. It was an elegant structure, inscribed with temperance precepts, and prayers and vows to the Virgin Mary. Almost the whole village, I was informed, had a few years before gone over to the society, and most of the *habitants* had taken the pledge for themselves and their children, and wore the "Temperance Cross." Some have even black temperance crosses hanging up in their houses. The Catholic clergy of Canada have promoted this movement very zealously, and partly by their influence, partly because a majority of the Canadian parliament was favourable to it, it has happened that restrictive regulations, similar to those of New England and many States of the Union, have been passed here in Canada.

Canada bears in many respects the same relation to the great Republic that Belgium does to France, and every movement and reform that takes place there is echoed on the St Lawrence. An enemy of the Catholic priests, with whom I afterwards spoke, explained their zeal in the cause of temperance, by saying, that they made it a new means of influence and "meddling in people's houses and families."

"The peasants have a great deal more to confess to them—that they have broken the pledge and got drunk; that they have vexed the Holy Virgin Mary, &c.—and then the priests have to inflict penances and punishments upon them."

Our complaisant *habitant* led us through all his farm-buildings and stables, and over his fields. He cultivated, like his neighbours everywhere about

Quebec, much barley, oats, and rye, and but little wheat, though there was some, and even some Indian corn. Probably this is to be seen nowhere else in the world where the climate is as severe as in Quebec, where not seldom the temperature is so low that even quicksilver is frozen. In Vermont, on Lake Champlain, indeed, much Indian corn is grown, and many African negroes are living, and yet there, though the latitude is that of Florence, quicksilver has frozen twice within the last forty years. Some few negroes are also to be found in Quebec, and that these children of the Sahara desert can endure such a climate is evidence of the extraordinary elasticity of nature in all human races. That Indian corn will grow here must be attributed to the heat of the short summer, which makes all vegetation as rapid as in Russia.

Monsieur Bienville, as a *gros habitant*, had everything on rather a grand scale, but most of the people have very miniature possessions, — little narrow strips of fields, on which they raise a little of everything, a little hay, a little wood, a little milk and butter from a cow; and all these little productions they carry themselves to the market in the town, sitting there patiently till they sell them. When they have sat twelve hours and earned two shillings they are quite content. "We," said a British colonist, " have not as much patience as is wanted for these petty dealings. We get a good large piece of land, and plough, and sow, and reap on steadily till we have a good load, and then we sell it all at once without losing much time or many words about it." Occasionally you hear in these Canadian villages of a stray German who has found his way here; I was told, for instance, of a certain *Monsieur Janquin,* the English called him Master Jenkins, and most likely his name was really Zinken; and there were some Germans whose names were given up in despair by both French and English as unpronounceable, and who were distinguished as " *le petit Allemand,*" or John the German. These people are said to be descendants of the notorious Hessian regiment which England called to her assistance in the revolutionary war, and whose fate can be traced in many parts of America over which they were scattered. Many of them came back to Europe, some remained in the Union, as, for instance, in Pennsylvania, where they sometimes exchanged the sword for the pen or the pedagogue's sceptre, and some were settled by the English Government in Canada, and found their way into the French villages, where they and their names became both Gallicised.

" *Northshire,*" that is, the north of the St Lawrence, is much more purely French than "*South-shire*," as it is called. In the south, the old French villages are mixed with British and American; or, as the Canadians say, "European" settlements (as if they themselves were aborigines of the country). On the northern shore of the river everything is much more in the old Canadian style, but towards the west the Canadian element declines as well as towards the south. This difference is seen also in the population of the two cities. In Quebec more than the half of the inhabitants are of French descent. According to the census of 1847 there were 22,000 French out of 37,000 inhabitants, and in society the French element is predominant; but in Montreal it does not play by any means so important a part. There the French are scarcely more than a third of the population, and the British are, politically, commercially, and socially, preponderant. Upper Canada is almost wholly Anglo-Saxon, and the whole province does not contain more French Canadians than the town of Quebec alone, that is, about 20,000, and these have been mostly only carried along with the great tide of Anglo-Saxon immigration.

The most completely French portion of all Canada is the north-eastern shore of the St Lawrence, from Quebec quite down to Labrador, and this is confirmed by the fact that the colonies lately carried from the St Lawrence to the great Saguenay river, and lake St John, were all French Canadians.

They have been hitherto much better acquainted with this country than the British, and it may be said that in the French time it was better known to the world at large than it has been since. The British have not yet quite re-discovered it, and in many of the localities of the lower St Lawrence, inhabited by pure Canadians, the state of things is described as quite that of the golden age. On the *Isle aux Coudres*, for example, which lies on the northern side of the river, sixty miles below Quebec, and is inhabited only by Canadians, there has never been a theft or any other crime known; and the people never fasten their doors, and live in the most perfect peace with one another. Even the cultivated French of Quebec live in a much more simple and primitive manner than the English,— rise early, dine at noon, and go to bed with the fowls. Luxury and extravagance, as well as comfort, have been brought into the country by the English.

At the western extremity of Canada, on Lake Superior, and near the source of the Mississippi, and on the Upper Ottawa, the Canadians are also at home. Where steamers and stage coaches cease,

Canadian *Voyageurs* and *Coureurs des Bois* supply their place, and undertake the post and carrying-trade over this fine wilderness. In general the British are more at home in the fertile and cultivated districts—the French Canadians in the wilder and more remote.

After being further entertained by our friendly host with some "*gòteaux*" and gossip, and some stories of the *Bótoilles que Napoléon avait gógnées*, we took leave of him, and continued our excursion to the Montmorency Falls. These celebrated Falls have the disadvantage of lying rather too near the high road, almost in its very dust. You drive along a level or very gradually ascending plateau from Quebec, alight in the middle of a village, and come immediately behind the houses on the ledge from which the river falls; this is rather prosaic. You wish to see a cataract come thundering down amidst wild and unknown mountain or forest regions, falling, possibly, from the clouds, or from some inaccessible glaciers, which feed it, though invisible, but the illusion is much diminished when you have gone down and examined it, and know the roads, and villages, and fields that are lying about it. Otherwise this Fall of Montmorency is a beautiful, lofty, abundant, concentrated mass of water and foam.

A little girl, completely deaf and dumb, and who

conversed with us in pantomime, accompanied us as our guide, and with her silent, but expressive and poetical language, increased our enjoyment, as much as the chatter of an ordinary guide would have diminished it. She took me gently by the arm, and placed me on the summit of the rock, close to where the water leaps over it; then she pointed with her long out-stretched finger below, to where the clouds of white foam were tinted by the sun with glorious hues of blue, red, and yellow, accompanying with light gestures their movement as they floated away in the air.

With the same quiet but earnest manner, springing over the rocks like a chamois, and watching and sharing our enthusiasm, she led us to several other points, and waved her arms upwards to the clouds, and downwards to the bottom of the fall, and then she tripped along a narrow foot-path, along which we followed her, as soon as we had divined her intention, which was to show us the fall from below. This is the principal scene. You follow the path for about half a mile down to the shores of the St Lawrence, turn to the left, and find yourself in a little river, bay, or cove, surrounded by rocky walls, and filled by the waters of the St Lawrence, like a tranquil little lake. At the bottom of this cove, which is filled and emptied by the tide, you see the fall. It is said that this is most beautiful in the winter; the little bay then freezes completely over, and you can walk on the ice quite up to the fall. In that season, which is in general in Canada the season of leisure, of enjoyment, and social pleasure (the short summer, when the navigation is open, must be used for something *better*)—in the winter this rocky valley is filled with brilliant sledges, skaters, and promenaders from Quebec, who enjoy the fresh air and the beautiful scenery in their favourite fashion. Even the cataract itself is then partly frozen, and makes with its immense icicles and columns an imposing appearance.

Exactly opposite the fall in the bay, lies a great black mass of rock, which has been thrown down in some convulsion, and round this the gorgeously-coloured clouds were forming a rainbow with most picturesque effect. In winter the spray settles as ice upon it, and then the block grows into a huge lofty glacier, and is sometimes turned to account by a gay party from Quebec, as a *montagne Russe*, or we might say Canadian—for this pleasure is just as much in vogue on the St Lawrence as at Moscow. The name it bears here is *Toboggening*, from an old Indian word, for the practice is also probably an Indian one. Small sledges made in the Indian fashion are called a *Toboggen;* they are made like their canoes, out of one piece, and barely afford room for a lady and gentleman.

I was surprised to hear, too, that the Europeans here have adopted another Indian invention, that of snow-shoes—though they may be regarded in some measure as a natural necessity of the country. The Indians and Canadians manage this inconvenient *chaussure* best, and can not only run but leap in it, and in the Canadian villages they have snow-shoe races. The snow falls here sometimes to such a depth, and remains so long on the ground, that even English ladies are obliged to accustom themselves to their troublesome method of locomotion, if they are not willing entirely to renounce fresh air and exercise. Many of them attain to great excellence in the art, and then they undertake long excursions and pleasure parties on snow-shoes, and not unfrequently something very much like a steeple-chase, when they display as much boldness and skill in crossing snow-covered hedges and ditches as their countrywomen in England in riding and hunting.

The Montmorency Fall may, on the whole, be regarded as a specimen of a kind very common here. At many points round the edge of the great rocky table-land of Labrador, similar waterfalls are found, pouring their streams into the sea, as here into the deep basin of the St Lawrence. Even to the north of Labrador and Hudson's Bay, on the coast of Melville Island, and other arctic regions of America, there are found rivers which fall from a height of three or four hundred feet into small deep ravine-like bays, and form—to judge from the descriptions of Parry, Franklin, and other arctic navigators—scenes precisely like that of the Falls of Montmorency. The geological formation which prevails so extensively in the north, might lead one to expect a similar geographical configuration of the country.

The "Water Privilege" of Montmorency formerly belonged to a French Seigneur, but now it and the Seigneurie have passed into the hands of an Englishman, who turns away a great part of the falling water to set a saw-mill in motion. We visited his establishment, which employs no less than 1500 people, who, besides the boards and planks, make doors and window-frames, and other component parts of houses, and are also occupied with the shipping of the vast piles of wood that come down to the lumber yard.

CHAPTER XVI.

THE INDIANS OF ST LORETTE.

WE now turned aside from the great road, and crossed the fields through several Canadian villages, to visit the Indian village of St Lorette. At St Pierre we heard that they had lately shot a large bear quite close to the houses. At St Michel we met a hunter, who had just come down from the mountain (the Laurentides), bringing with him on a cart a large elk, and two of the small Canadian hares, called here wild cats (*châts de forêts*). He had no other weapon than a clumsy old flint gun. The French peasants, whom we saw, were going about their houses in great, thick, heavy sabots, like those seen in Champagne and Westphalia, and thick woollen night-caps hanging down long over their backs; even those whom we met in carts or on horse-back had not laid aside their beloved night-caps; and it must be owned that these wooden-shoed and night-capped Canadians do in America look very anti-progressive. The Germans have mostly laid aside their old European dress, so that it would seem that the French are more wedded to old customs than any other nation settled here.

I have often had occasion to mention Indian customs and material objects, the Pipe of Peace, the canoe, &c., which have been introduced among the Canadian French; and I found that the old Indian national dish called *Sagamité*, so often mentioned in the earliest reports of the Jesuits, is a favourite among the Canadian peasants. What the word means I have in vain inquired, but the dish consists of maize boiled in milk; though the poor Indians probably boiled it for their Jesuit Fathers in water; and since it formed for a hundred years the daily bread of so many pious missionaries in the wilderness, there is a kind of historical interest attached to it. It is often met with at the tables of respectable citizens in Montreal and Quebec.

In these Quebec villages the trees were almost leafless, though in the island of Montreal they still bore a rich, many-coloured foliage; and in the more feebly developed fruit trees in the gardens the same influence of the northern climate was observable. The fine fruit of Montreal is not found here, and of the magnificent apples called *fumeuses*, which grow there, we had brought with us on the steamer a whole cargo to Quebec.

As we approached the village of Lorette, and the wind blew rather cold from the mountains, we met two men in an open cart sitting with their backs to the horse, and leaving him to find his way as he best might. "Those are queer drivers," I remarked to my French coachman.

"Yes, sir, they are Irishmen," he answered laconically, as if that accounted for anything. These two Paddies were returning from the city to their village, one of the Irish back settlements that extend behind those of the French into the interior of the country.

At St Lorette we first went to visit the schoolmaster, whom we found on duty, that is, in the midst of his brown pupils. He himself was, as he told us, a Huron, and I was rather surprised that he, a cultivated man, so readily acknowledged his savage origin. It would have been quite another thing if he had come of an African race. A mulatto or a quadroon will only mention his white blood, but no one in Canada has any hesitation in saying, "I am a Huron, an Iroquois, or a Mohawk." These races were destroyed or driven out by the Europeans, but never reduced to slavery, and only the submitting to a yoke of this kind seems to be everywhere regarded as the forfeiture of national honour. No one blushes for being merely wild and barbarous, and in civilized China, for example, the nobles think a descent from the Mantchoo Tartars a cause for boasting.

The sight of the little Indian school-children interested me in the highest degree. We had before us the most various mixtures of European and Indian blood, and although the children were all called Indians, some of them were as fair and rosy-cheeked as Europeans. Some however had the brown faces and harsh coal-black hair of the pure Iroquois. The boys were mostly much handsomer and better made than the girls, and they, as well as their masters, were always able to tell from what race they were descended. Most of them were Hurons, as nearly the whole colony of St Lorette is, but some were Algonquins, some Abenakis, and others Iroquois, and there were also a few Amalekites, or Micmacs from New Brunswick. All these once powerful and dreaded tribes have dwindled almost to atoms, and it is remarkable that these atoms are still so well informed as to their character and origin. The school-master told me that among the Indian villages in Canada, few and widely scattered as they are, a tolerably active intercourse is maintained. An Indian of Upper Canada, or New Brunswick, or Nova Scotia, should his affairs bring him to Quebec, seldom fails to pay a visit to the men of his race at St Lorette, and thence arise frequently marriages or other connections, which account for the circumstance that the offspring of so many other tribes are to be found here.

The little Indians, at our request and the command of their master, now set up a song, and it was really a terrific performance. It seemed as if they were all going to fly at us at once, it was a regular storm, and the impression made on us was very much what other travellers have described from the war-whoop, and yet it was intended for a pious French hymn. They certainly kept time, however, and if it had not been for the very war-like character of their religious exercise, there would have been no fault to find with it. The free and bold attitude of the youngsters also struck me, most of them stood erect with folded arms, and trumpeted out their hymn with all the strength of their lungs. The instruction is given in French, and their books and the pupils' copies seemed all very orderly and neatly kept.

The schoolmaster had the kindness afterwards to take us to some of the families in the village, and

I was not a little astonished at the order and cleanliness I found in the houses. Many a farmer's house in France and England could not be compared with those of the Hurons, and in many parts of Scotland and Germany the comparison might put the Europeans to shame.

The "First Chief" of the village was not at home, so we visited the "Second Chief," who had a whole house full of children, and introduced us to his aged, but still quite active father, whom we found digging in his garden.

"You are very industrious in your garden," said I, when I had been presented.

"Pooh! pooh!" said he smiling, but throwing away his spade contemptuously, "I must dig and work in the fields now, but formerly I went hunting, and shot moose deer, and bears. That was much better. *Mais v'là, à présent je fais le laboureur. C'est détéstable.*" These Indians do not seem to be of the opinion of the Romans, who regarded agriculture as a noble occupation, even for the conquerors of the world. Their whole genius appears to be interwoven with the life of the forests and hunting-grounds, and though they have now been cultivating the ground for so many years, their dreams are still of the wilderness.

We were now led into the house and presented

by our host to his wife, an old Norna-like figure, wrapped in a large black shawl, and sitting silent and motionless by the fire. He mentioned her name, but I have forgotten it; he himself was, he informed us, called by an Indian appellation signifying, "I have a river in my mouth," given to him by flatterers in his younger days because he had shown some signs of eloquence. These people were in their dress and persons, as well as in their habitations, as clean and orderly as could be desired. They showed us some pretty embroidery with elk's hair upon elk's leather, &c., and with porcupine quills upon birch bark, which was really very tasteful, and which they offered for sale. Mr "I-have-a-river-in-my-mouth" seemed indeed to carry on quite a wholesale trade in them, for he had great tuns and chests full of mocassins embroidered with flowers, cigar-cases, purses, &c., all made by the women in the village, and which were, I believe, destined to be sent to Montreal, and thence probably to Niagara and New York. This interesting little branch of industry flourishes, I believe, in all the Indian colonies of Canada.

These Indians, educated and civilized as they are, do not yet devote themselves wholly to the peaceful occupations of the garden and the field. "Our restless young men," said our host, "wander every year, for four or five weeks, to the north, live in huts or tents in the woods, go hunting in the old fashion, and return with their game at an appointed time to the village. Many of us are in the service of the Hudson's Bay Company, and follow the chase in the regions round Hudson's Bay, and these do not perhaps return to the village till they feel themselves growing old."

He mostly spoke of the people of the village of St Lorette as "The Huron nation," as if these few hundred men were all the remains of that once mighty race. "Our nation," he said, "receives every year from the Queen of England certain presents of weapons, powder, and provisions, and when my son and a brother-chief goes to receive them from the Commissioner, he always presents himself in his full costume as an Indian chief, and carries on the business in the name of the 'Huron nation.'" The old man showed us this official full dress of his son, but he himself, like all peaceful Hurons, was dressed like a Canadian peasant, minus the night-cap and the wooden shoes, which the Indians have not adopted. Not far from St Lorette, and near the limits of the cultivated valley of the St Lawrence, scarcely sixty miles from Quebec, there are still some quite wild Indians, called by the French *Montagnois*, but they are few, poor, and widely scattered. They live by hunting and fishing, and are mostly found in isolated family groups in the forests, which they leave as seldom as the bears. A few years ago I was told nine of these *Montagnois* took the resolution of coming for the first time to see St Lorette and Quebec, and pitched their tents near their countrymen, going from time to time to the city, where they were regarded as almost as much curious novelties as they would have been thought in Europe, although, as I have said, their usual habitations are not sixty miles off.

On our return to Quebec, when some of the most distinguished naturalists in America were in our company, we heard, during a conversation relating to whites and red-skins, that the American wild plants disappear before European weeds, just as the aborigines do before the immigrants. Wherever the Europeans come, they say, there immediately springs up a European vegetation, which takes root energetically, and drives out that native to the country. In many cases, of course, this admits of explanation, as when Europeans sow various kinds of corn from the old world, it is very conceivable that they may also sow the seeds of many weeds; but sometimes there does really appear something almost mysterious in the process. When, for example, Europeans pass only once through the forest or district previously peopled only by Indians, and make their bivouac fire and their night quarters there, the place is thenceforward marked by the springing up of European wild plants. Railroads have been carried across regions hitherto untrodden; and along the line sprouted forth, not American, but new European weeds.

"The Indians," said my esteemed informant, "have long made the same remark, and have given to a weed commonly appearing under such circumstances (the English Plantain, or *Plantago Major*) the name of 'the White Man's Footstep.'"

The last rays of the sun were shining on the tin-covered roofs when we got back to Quebec—those roofs which have procured for Montreal the name of the "Silver Town," and produced a most magical effect. Many of the towers which were half in shadow glowed as if ignited, and I am convinced that if an old Spanish *Conquistador* had seen them, he would have sent off the most glowing accounts of a city on the St Lawrence, built entirely of gold and silver.

CHAPTER XVII.

THE QUEBEC SEMINARY.

I PASSED an instructive and interesting morning in the Catholic College of Quebec, one of the oldest and most remarkable institutions of the country, which has been, for 200 years, with the "Seminary," at the head of the education of the Canadian clergy, and the Catholic youth in general. It was founded in 1663 by François de Laval, the first Bishop of Quebec, its original destination being merely for the clergy, and it was as richly endowed as the Seminary of Montreal. A tax of one-thirteenth on all the produce of the earth was imposed for its support, but, as this was thought exorbitant, and excited great discontent in the colony, it was after a time lowered to a twenty-sixth. Like the Montreal Seminary, it is divided into a *Grand* and *Petit Seminaire*,—in the first of which study about

40 young theologians, and in the second 400 young people, receive general education.

The greater part of the pupils are *Pensionnaires*, and reside in the institution; the rest are *externes*, and receive only instruction. The great majority of them are of French origin, but there are also English, Irish, British Canadians, and even Americans from the United States. The fewest are from Quebec itself, and it cannot therefore be considered as a mere town school, but as an institution for America at large. I found half a dozen young men from Boston alone, many from Upper Canada, and some from New Brunswick. There were some Englishmen among the heads of the Seminary and teachers, and altogether about sixty of British families. Probably the good education given, and the low charge made for it, may induce the English to send their children to this old French establishment; for a young man can, I was told, be maintained and instructed for from thirty to forty guineas. The school is divided into an upper class for "Rhetoric and Philosophy," a lower "*Classe Préparatoire*," and between these there are six others. Besides these the scholars are assembled in many private classes and societies, which exist in addition to the official ones, and which are conducted under the superintendence of the teachers, by the pupils themselves, who seek to excite each other's emulation.

Among these is an *Académie de St Denys*, founded in 1822, "to animate zeal, and reward industry and progress." It consists 1st of 20 *Académiciens*, chosen from the philosophy and rhetoric classes—2nd, of the so-called *Candidates* from the middle; and 3rdly, of Aspirants who may be taken from the lowest and most elementary. The qualifications for the members of this Academy are, that they shall have gained some principal prize—"*premier prix d' excellence;* "—or have been in general remarkably successful; and, secondly, that they shall be of pious and blameless conduct.

The second Private Society among the pupils is the *Société Laval*, founded in 1851, in honour of the bishop of that name. It is especially for the middle classes, and the President, Vice-President, and Secretary of it are pupils; and their sittings are devoted to the communication of written essays, to discussion, declamation, and the solution of grammatical and literary questions. The third is the *Société Typographique*, dating from 1848, and choosing its officers from the upper classes. It publishes a journal which has two editors, and appears twice a week in small folio; and which is written, composed, printed, and sold by the scholars. It bears the title of the "Bee," with the motto, "*Je suis chose légère, et vais de fleur en fleur,*" and has already existed six years, and fills six volumes. It contains a series of excellent and useful extracts from good writers—for instance, one from Lord Bacon, "On Conversation;" "On Early Education," from *L'amie de la Religion;* a little article by the "*Modeste Abeille,*" "*Contre l'Ours du Nord, et sa griffe meurtrière qu'il étend vers Constantinople,*"—a good little paper in which the Bee, "*parceque son foible bourdonnement ne pourra pas faire taire la guerre,*" undertakes (long before the battles near Sebastopol) to register the Wars of the Giants; a Eulogium on Silvio Pellico; geographical and historical essays; replies to questions mooted within the Quebec Seminary; and, lastly, a touching *necrologe* on the death of two distinguished pupils of another Canadian Seminary, Hyacinth College, on the Yamaska (a small tributary of the St Lawrence, eastward of Montreal), to which the students of Quebec had recently paid a visit during their vacation.

The Journal contained a very ample and well-written account of the journey, the description of one half of Canada, by a young Canadian patriot. The visitors had been addressed at the college on the Yamaska by a Monsieur Adolph Jaques, one of the most distinguished students, in the name of his fellows, and replied to by a M. Marmet for the guests. He was at that time Editor of the "Bee," and the former one of its most zealous correspondents; and it happened that both these promising young men were carried off by death, nearly at the same time,—"*tous deux chargés de la même mission, tous deux honorés et chéris de leurs confrères, tous deux doués de talents remarquables, et couronnés de lauriers à la fin de chaque année scolaire.*"

What a store of recollections must this little Bee be laying up for the later years of the students: the history, not only of their early lives, but of their youthful ideas. At the end of the present century, some grey-haired man who had been brought up here, need only ask for a yearly volume of this little periodical, to transport himself back to the days of his youth. And what enjoyment, what useful, practical, and encouraging hints may not the young people engaged in it at present receive!

The idea of a typographical society alone, for the practice of an art so intimately connected with literature and science, is excellent and suitable. Should not every scholar have some knowledge of the art of printing, as well as of writing?

I should like to hear what our German schoolmen would say to these Canadian institutions. The name of Canada awakens in our minds ideas of wild barbarians rather than of educational institutions. "What good thing can come out of Canada?" might they ask. Quebec, situated at the extreme limit of the civilised world, seems little likely to be a centre of intellectual movement; and we Protestants of Saxony and Prussia would not be inclined to look to a Seminary under the guidance of the Catholic clergy for new and valuable ideas of reform.

Have we Saxons and Prussians, with our much-praised school-system, which assuredly is in many respects good, yet set in motion the lever so much employed at Quebec—that of private emulation among the scholars,—the lever of free and voluntary association for the glorious objects of education,—the lever of voluntary effort, and of non-official rewards? The praise, the rewards, the prizes distributed by the authorities for appointed tasks, are certainly good, necessary, and indispensable; but do they not tend in some measure to encourage servility? How delightful is the free acknowledgment of our merit from equals of our own class and standing—our "Peers."

How encouraging and beneficial must such motives and such a field for free exertion be to young men of sturdily independent character, who are so apt to get into collision with school regulations and school tasks, arbitrarily imposed, and in consequence of such collisions often become unruly and idle, but who are not irreclaimable. Many a headstrong spirit of this sort has, by being enabled first to distinguish himself in these private voluntary associations, been ultimately reconciled to the regular school-system. They may even serve a useful purpose to the teachers themselves, who must naturally be a little inclined to despotic authority, and to an obstinate persistence in their own plans; even to them it may serve as a wholesome opposition, and call their attention to much that they might otherwise overlook.

When they find perhaps some young genius,—of whom they have made little account, or even rejected,—recognised and distinguished by his fellows, they may be led to take him by the hand and bring him forward for his own and others' good.

I feel that I am expressing myself awkwardly, but the reader may perceive my meaning, to develope which fully would require a more lengthened discussion. He will see that I wish to suggest the inquiry, whether we German Protestants might not in some things take example by the Roman Catholic college of Canada, and encourage at our high schools similar private societies, and courts of honour—at least in some modified form? I will not undertake to decide the question, but I could not help feeling, along with my approval and admiration of what I saw of the students and their teachers at Quebec, an emotion of regret that nothing of the kind had existed at the institutions at which I was myself educated.

The "Presidents" of these societies, and the Editors of the Bee, showed us with great zeal over their typographical establishments, and the Professors led us through the various departments of the extensive buildings, in which there are apartments for corporeal and mental exercises, a library of 12,000 volumes, and a richly-furnished cabinet of physical science, such as I should be glad to see in every German gymnasium. Many of the improvements are still recent, but they are making rapid progress, and it may not be long before we shall find that we might get many good hints on these things from both Lower and Upper Canada.

In one department of this old Seminary I found the remainder of the lately burnt library of the Canadian parliament. Fires are throughout Canada, as well as the United States, a real plague, and not only stores and private dwellings, but literary and scientific collections are constantly threatened by them. The Quebec Seminary has twice suffered much from fire, and of the Quebec Parliament library more than 9000 volumes were burnt out of 18,000, and amongst them the celebrated *Relations des Jesuites*—the most complete collection ever made of them. In Montreal, where also the Parliament House was burnt down some years ago, 30,000 volumes were consumed, and both these fires took place a short time before the conflagration which destroyed the Congress Library at Washington. A very complete collection of objects of Canadian natural history were also consumed in the fire of Quebec, and I saw in a small room all that was saved, a few stuffed animals and other objects, presented by the Quebec Historical Society. I could never fully understand the causes of the extraordinary prevalence of this scourge, which in those countries is more inimical to scientific collections than moths or rust.

I sought in vain in the libraries of Quebec (including the small one of the Historical Society) for ancient maps of the country, or original documents bearing on the oldest history of Canada. They do not exist here: everything of interest is a copy from Paris; so my researches in this department proved somewhat futile. I was, however, glad to see that here, as well as throughout America, much more attention is now devoted to these subjects than formerly.

Very lately the Canadian government sent a young man to Paris, and he returned with a number of excellent copies of ancient maps of Canada; and old Jaques Cartier, the Columbus of Canada, the first discoverer and navigator of the great St Lawrence, who bestowed names on it, and the country, I found now held in universal honour. To this the Literary and Historical Societies of Quebec have doubtless contributed; under their direction was published in 1843 a new critical work on the first arrival of Europeans in Canada, *(Voyages de découverte au Canada entre les années 1534—1542,)* and the learned Canadian historians MM. Fariboult and Garneau have contributed much, by their admirable works, to promote the study of history.

Particular points of antiquarian interest, such as at what part of the river Cartier first landed, where he wintered, &c.,—have been treated in pamphlets published by the above societies; and an old gun found near Quebec, on the often mentioned river St Charles, the rudder of an old ship's boat, &c., gave occasion to some curious discussions; a particular Memoir of the said cannon was issued under the name of " *Le Canon de Bronze.*"

The old and almost forgotten names of Cartier, Stadacone (the Indian name for Quebec), Hochelaga (the Indian name for Montreal), Agouhanna (a Chief near Quebec), Donnacona (an Indian Cacique near Montreal,) &c., were as if raised from the grave, and became so current in Canada, that a popular and esteemed author could bestow the name of Hochelaga on his work, and be everywhere understood. Many hundreds of copies were made of a representation of the old French *habitation* on the site of the present citadel of Quebec, and, in 1847, the town of St Malo sent to Canada a copy of the well-preserved portrait of the brave old knight Cartier, which was engraved, and the engravings sold by thousands. There came also from France a drawing of the ancestral abode in Bretagne— the *habitation* of this remarkable man, the house in which he was born and died, and a copy of a picture of his first arrival in Canada. Since then his name has penetrated everywhere; streets and "*Places*" have been named after him in Montreal and Quebec, and a steamer I lately saw was called the "Jaques Cartier." A popular biography however, like that of Columbus by Washington Irving, has not yet been written of the Canadian Conquistador.

CHAPTER XVIII.

MISCELLANIES.

My friends were kind enough to take me sometimes to the Canadian Parliament, and I found there at all times of the day life, movement, and society. It seemed to me as if its doors stood open the whole day, like the approaches to the old Forum Romanum, where some kind of discussion was always going on, even when "Senatus Populusque" were not assembled.

Early in the morning I found many members already in their places, corresponding, reading, turning over papers, and taking notes, and always some groups engaged in conversation. A large reading-room, in which all the political journals of Canada, England, and the United States, were to be found, is as inseparable a part of this political exchange as of the commercial in another part of the town. Here people are going in and out the whole day, making appointments, forming committees, &c., and in the evening there was a sitting which I was allowed to attend. On the table of the House lay a Mace, precisely like that of the English Parliament; will any American Cromwell ever cry "Take away that bauble"? The members here, as in England, bow to the Speaker, called *l' Orateur*, when they pass his table, and the official attendants, the sergeant-at-arms, ushers, &c., are similar; but it struck me as peculiar that the trifling services of the Parliament, the carrying messages, letters, &c., or waiting on the commands of the Speaker, were performed by young half-grown lads. They were dressed in black, and contributed something to the picturesque effect of the scene, as they sat or lay, when they were not wanted, on the carpeted steps leading to the Speaker's chair.

Of the debates which were carried on, partly in English, partly in French, I did not understand much. So much however I made out, that there were present a lately fallen ministry, and a triumphant present one (nothing uncommon in Canada), and that the fallen one was exposed to a vehement and bitter attack from a very zealous but crotchety member on the extreme left. They were accused of want of economy in the management of the public money, and a committee of inquiry was appointed. This committee, and the mode of its formation, appeared suspicious to that ultra-democratic member. In a long and violent speech he declared it a " White-washing Committee," and endeavoured to show that it was so constituted as to make the acquittal of the ministry a matter of course. He did not hesitate to cast on gentlemen present the coarsest accusations of appropriating money to their own private advantage, and painted their whole conduct in the blackest colours. Of this phrase, " White-washing Committee," he appeared so enamoured that he repeated it about once a minute, in a speech of two hours' length. The passionate little gentleman had no sooner ceased than he was attacked on all sides. He had been, I heard, driven from several Canadian Parliaments, but always managed somehow to slip in again, and he was given to understand, with all sorts of piquant variations, that, as a journalist, he vilified every mortal but himself; that he lived in enmity with God and man; that he was the very incarnation of selfishness, and that his little pug nose was always scenting out something dirty, except in himself, where it was oftenest to be found. I was astounded at the uncompromising hard words with which he was pelted, but they seemed to trouble him very little. He sat at his desk looking perfectly unconcerned, turning over some papers, apparently engaged, like a little god of love, in sharpening fresh arrows, and now and then looking with a malicious smile over his shoulder in the faces of his angry assailants. I could not help thinking however, from his physiognomy (if Lavater is at all to be trusted), that, should he ever attain to power, he might need a " White-washing Committee" quite as much as those whom he had been denouncing.

A pleasant contrast is afforded by passing from such a parliamentary debate as this to a gay *Soirée Dansante*, where the very men who have just been standing front to front on the field of apparently ferocious conflict, now appear pacified and smiling, deporting themselves to one another like gentlemen, in a kind of half-glorified state, as we may hope it will be in that world where we shall have left our earthly quarrels, grudges, and angry passions behind us. Long live *soirées*, for they certainly help to " strew life's path with fragrant flowers."

It was the first large party of the winter, what one might call the opening of the season, that I had thus the good fortune to attend, and all the " beauty and fashion" of Quebec was assembled on the occasion; but one of my chief pleasures was to see the cordial intermingling of the two great West

European nationalities, which had lately been so chivalrously maintaining the freedom of Europe before Sebastopol. French grace and Anglo-Saxon manliness, or, if I may be allowed the word, *gentlemanliness*, danced and jested, and hovered from room to room; and in the midst of the guests appeared, well pleased, the noble-minded and highly cultivated man who then ruled the country from Lake Superior to Newfoundland and Labrador.

The society of Quebec is really, in animation, spirit, and refinement, inferior to that of no other capital in the world, and I wish I could convey to the reader some idea of the sparkling and even instructive conversation that this pleasant evening afforded me, but it would be like attempting to catch and paint the bubbles in a foaming glass of champagne. The "wise," for whom "half a word" is sufficient, will easily understand that I carried home with me most agreeable recollections of the Quebec opening *soirée*, and retired to an excellent night's rest to the before-mentioned little wooden cell in which I, and some more distinguished travellers, had to deposit our individuality in the first hotel of Quebec.

CHAPTER XIX.

FROM QUEBEC TO MONTREAL.

On our return passage up the river night covered the beautiful part of the St Lawrence that we had previously seen by daylight; but, on the other hand, the sun showed us much that had been previously hidden in darkness. Both passages together afforded us a complete view of the whole renowned and glorious water. The whole evening through we saw both shores lit up by the lights in the long rows of houses in the St Lawrence villages; it was like a hundred miles long street illumination. Among the passengers was a young priest, with whom I soon got into talk. He had been hitherto the pastor of a little flock in the neighbourhood of Gaspé Bay, in the district of Gaspésié at the mouth of the St Lawrence, and he gave me a lively and touching description of the simple lives of the poor fisher population, and of their doings on land and ocean, which last is their granary and store-room, and, from the accounts of my informant, I was led to infer that the part of Lower Canada that I had not seen, the part below Quebec, and on both sides of the vast sea-like river, was one of the greatest interest for an ethnographer and a philanthropist. But what I could not see I was glad to hear of. A traveller more favourably circumstanced who may think to make this journey, must take notice that he will have to land at Gaspé, and make his way for 200 miles along the rough, iron-bound south coast, from village to village, to Quebec, and then back again for 500 miles, along the still more rugged northern coast to Bellisle, where the last French settlements are lost in the country of the Montagnois and Esquimaux. This he must do if he wishes to boast that he knows anything of true Lower Canada.

My good companion, I learned, had lately been transplanted from the region of the cod-fishes, where he had so long been fishing for souls, to another part of Canada, a settlement in a valley beyond the first range of hills in the neighbourhood of *Trois Rivières*. He expected to find a mixed flock of French and Irish, and was, he said, quite prepared for the contingency, as he could preach in English as well as in his native language. The French clergy here generally find a knowledge of English quite necessary on account of the great numbers of Irish emigrants, who do not bring with them a corresponding number of priests; and it is therefore taught at the seminary of Quebec in preference to all other languages. I did nevertheless meet with several French priests who did not speak a word of English, and I need hardly say that very few of the French peasants do.

My companion spoke with great interest of the old songs and hymns that the French Canadians preserved among them, and which they were in the habit of singing at their social gatherings. I had heard before of these popular poems, hymns, and *Romances*, that had been brought hither from Normandy, Brittany, and La Vendée, and which in France itself had been in a great measure forgotten. Even the Canadian boatmen on the Upper Mississippi, are acquainted, as a gentleman living among them informed me, with many pretty *chansons, refrains, barcaroles, rondes*, &c., which they give with precisely the same airs and the same words as their ancestors of 300 years ago. I afterwards gave myself a good deal of trouble to procure some of these boasted popular melodies in Montreal, and bought all the printed collections I could find, but they did not equal my expectations; I did not find in them the treasure of popular poetry I looked for, on the contrary, few of them bore the genuine stamp of antiquity, or of a popular origin; they were unfortunately of a very mixed character. There were some collections, called by such names as *La Lyre Canadienne*, that contained French poems of the present day, the "*Parisienne*," "*Varsovienne*," &c.; and some of those specially entitled "*Chansons Canadien*" were only so called because they referred to Canada, or were by some young Canadian priest.

It was, nevertheless, interesting to me to find that the poetical blossoms springing up on the soil of France were immediately transferred to the St Lawrence, as it showed that the sympathies of the people are still with the mother-country, as those of the Germans in the Baltic provinces of Russia are with Germany.

The class of Canadians most devoted to poetry and song are the *Voyageurs*—hunters and fur-traders, who pass the greater part of their lives in wandering through the most distant regions of Canada; and I found in my collections that the songs distinguished as "*Chant de Voyageur Canadien*," had more originality and a more popular character than the rest. They are easily recognised, and almost all begin with the idea of a return to their father's farm-yard, their sister's flower-garden, or their mother's room. I have, for example, three now lying before me, one of which begins:

> "Par derrière, chez mon père,
> Vole mon cœur, vole, vole, vole,
> Par derrière, chez mon père,
> Il y a un pommier doux, &c."

The second:

> "Par derrière, chez ma tante,
> Il y a un bois joli,
> Le rossignol y chante,
> Et le jour et la nuit, &c."

And the third in the same fashion:

> "Derrière, chez nous y a un étang,
> Derrière, chez nous y a un étang,
> Trois beaux canards s'en vont baignant
> Legèrement—legèrement, &c."

This *Derrière chez nous* does not mean, I presume, "behind our house," but rather "down there in our country;" a *Voyageur* of the North-West might be supposed to look back fondly to his far-off Canadian home.

When we parted for the night I had almost a quarrel with my good Canadian priest because I could not understand his last remark. He said, "*Lo nuict ä bien noaere*—which phrase, though he repeated it several times, I could by no means make out. At last he naturally got impatient, and could not see why his pronunciation made the darkness of his remark equal to that of the night; to which, as the reader will perceive, he meant to point my attention.

The morning that followed too, though certainly not black or *noaere*, was at least dark grey. A thick mist had settled on the river, so that we had to come to anchor in the middle of it, near the town of *Trois Rivières*, which lies exactly midway between Quebec and Montreal, at the entrance to Lake St Peter's, and at the mouth of the great St Maurice river, and is in population and general importance the third town of Lower Canada. I found here, too, one German settler, and it appeared to me that this one German settler was as standing a figure in the small places in Canada as the "one Cossack killed" in the Russian War bulletins. In Quebec and Montreal the number of my countrymen was rather more considerable; in the former there are fifty, in Montreal twice as many, but they are mostly only German Jews, engaged in the fur trade.

I visited some of them, and found, to my great surprise, that they dealt not only in Canadian, but also in Polish, Russian, and Siberian furs, which they imported from the Leipsig fair. One would certainly suppose Canada had enough of this article, and needed not to buy it from Russia and Germany. In Russia I had been formerly struck by the fact that they import and highly esteem the furs of Canada, and that the Hudson's Bay Company find Russia, herself so rich in furs, its best customer. Perhaps the explanation may be found in this, that though the wearing of furs is in these countries a necessity, it is also a matter of luxury and taste; and that two fur-producing countries may value and wish to possess each other's goods, just as two others may desire to exchange their respective productions in literature and art.

The delay from the fog had at least this advantage for us,—that it enabled us to see the St Lawrence from *Trois Rivières* upwards by daylight; and I was most interested by Lake St Peter's, here formed by the St Lawrence. It spreads out into a broad delta, with a countless number of arms, and between them an equal number of flat longish islands. In proportion as the islands are flat, the branches of the river are shallow; and as this is the flattest region on the whole St Lawrence, this is the place where the first ice forms in the winter.

First there comes a ring round each of the islands; then the smaller channels close, and by degrees the whole delta is frozen fast, and the bridge of ice is usually complete before Christmas. As soon as it is solid, it increases rapidly, as it stops the ice drifting down the river, and the freezing process then goes on backwards to Montreal, and it takes generally but a few days for the whole St Lawrence, from Lake St Peter's to Montreal, to become solid ice. Whoever wishes to know more of the winter phenomena of the St Lawrence may consult the works of the deservedly celebrated Canadian geologist, Mr W. E. Logan. The various reports concerning the building of the great Montreal railway bridge (the Victoria Bridge), contain some very interesting observations and results, concerning the character of the St Lawrence.

There is scarcely any other river in the world that exhibits such a variety of conditions in the water, and in the configurations of its bed. The Mississippi, the Danube, the Wolga, and most of the gigantic rivers of the world, are monotonous compared with it. They form broader or narrower channels, and the water flows in different parts with a more or less rapid current; but in the St Lawrence you scarcely find fifty miles that maintain the same character, and do not differ essentially from other sections of the river. It spreads out sometimes into a smaller, sometimes to a larger, lake, and these lakes are very numerous, and all various in depth and other circumstances. Some are like great deep ravines; others resemble broad inundations of a low country; sometimes the river rushes along in a cataract, at others creeps languidly through a wide marshy delta; is now a calm river, and now a gigantic mountain-torrent foaming for miles over a rocky bed. Several times along its course it divides into many branches, always under different circumstances, and its long trumpet-shaped mouth, which is half river half sea, is like that of no other river.

As soon as we had passed Lake St Peter's, we began to make up for lost time by racing with another steamer. It is very exciting sport, and though it may be dangerous, every passenger is so eager about it, and so strongly interested for his own boat, that one would think the most insignificant of them had a hundred dollars at stake in it. In British Canada these races are, I believe, forbidden, and occasionally punished; and they certainly do not cause so much mischief as in the United States. But, probably, they cannot be altogether prevented, any more than duels.

It must not be imagined that in these contests the vessels remain at a proper distance from each other, and leave each other room for manœuvring; if this were done the race would be prolonged, and many a good opportunity of distancing your rival lost. They come at the very beginning of the race quite close to each other, like two knights who want to tilt each other out of the saddle. Their two jib-booms make an acute angle, as though watching for an opportunity to pierce each other's sides, and the chimneys, instead of the usual black smoke, send forth a thick yellow vapour—for the captains have given orders to strew on the fire some pulverized colophonium, which is kept ready for the express purpose. This substance when sprinkled on the coals makes them burn more fiercely, and occasions a greater production of steam and greater motive power.

The two boats go tearing on for miles side by side, as if they were fastened together, and sometimes one or the other falls a little back. The channel is perhaps not broad, and then it may be you can manage to push your rival aside, and that he slackens a little for fear of running on rocks, or on a sand-bank. You instantly pursue your advantage, get up all your steam, on with some more colophonium, and make a spring under the very nose of your rival—who must now give in somewhat, for fear of a collision. You then get before him, and cut him off, and when he has once seen the stern of your vessel, he need no longer think of overtaking you. The affair is over, and away you go, soon far in advance, and triumphantly enter as winner the harbour of Montreal.

CHAPTER XX.

THE OTTAWA.

The Ottawa is the largest tributary of the St Lawrence, and it is also, from its geographical position, the most important. The east and west course of the main stream is continued by it, while the upper St Lawrence bears more to the south. The Ottawa is the shortest water route to the great upper lakes, and has, therefore, served from the earliest times more than the upper St Lawrence as the high-road to the West. Lake Superior, Lake Huron, and the Georgian Bay were discovered by means of the valley of the Ottawa, and most of the Jesuit missionaries passed up this valley, and reached thus the western branches of those inland seas.

The canal route of the Ottawa was, as early as the first quarter of the seventeenth century, one of the best known navigation lines of Canada, though subsequently it was from various causes much neglected; so much indeed that at the present moment many parts of it, and especially its sources, are nearly unknown, but steamers and railroads are now active in restoring the Ottawa country to its natural importance. It will become once more what it was at first—a great road to the West—but in a much higher degree.

That it is at the same time a new country, and the scene of old and primitive undertakings, made it so attractive to me that I determined on an excursion to Bytown,* the capital of the country.

I went first to "La Chine," the principal port of Montreal for all vessels going up the Ottawa. The rapids of St Louis interrupt the navigation, at least for upward-bound vessels, and you make a circuit by land to reach La Chine, where the water is again deep and tranquil. A railroad and a canal lead thither by the most direct route, but we preferred taking a carriage and driving along the old road, in order to enjoy the sight of the water-falls.

The whole mighty river here divides itself between rocks and islands into a number of wildly foaming torrents, but with high water the steamers

* Since named Ottawa, where the Prince of Wales, on his recent visit, laid the first stone of the House of Parliament.

coming down venture the passage, and a very interesting one it is said to be. In our little chaise however we got so close to the rapids that it was nearly as good. The road was very lonely and ran on the very edge of the water, and we often had, before and behind and on either side of us, roaring waves, black foam-covered rocks and wooded islands, with here and there glimpses of distant water, and at last the church tower and the white cottages of the Indian village of Koknawaga, or St Louis, which lies exactly opposite to La Chine. That Indians should have remained so long at this point, is probably to be ascribed to the existence of the cataract. The Indian natives were the first guides of European ships through this dangerous labyrinth, and they are still the best pilots to be found here. They are not only acquainted with every rock and shallow, and the state of the river at various seasons of the year, out they have peculiarly the quick eye and the energetic hand required to turn the arrow-like course of a ship from a danger which is perhaps only indicated by a spot of rather darker colour in the water. Many of the pilots on these waters are to this day Indians of Koknawaga.

La Chine, though only a village, is one of the oldest and most famous places in Canada. Its name is a memorial of the time when it was still supposed that the St Lawrence was one of the shortest ways to China, and that Montreal and Quebec were destined to become the chief staple places for Chinese goods, and the little harbour of La Chine was to be the place where they were first deposited. These hopes were not fulfilled, but the extraordinary name of the village has remained as a memento of the geographical error. During the flourishing period of the old French fur trade, La Chine was the rendezvous of the voyageurs and Canadian hunters, and their little fleets of canoes, in which they brought down their furs from the north-west. Here was the end of their journey, for their wares were here unshipped for Montreal. Here the Indian chiefs were received and rewarded, and hither came the "*Ononthios*," or French governors, to listen to their speeches, say something pretty in return, and conclude treaties of peace or commerce with them, and much the same thing is going on at the present day.

A great number of the French raft-men on the Ottawa come from La Chine, and you see loitering about, along with the Indian pilots of Koknawaga, voyageurs from the north-west, for whom La Chine is a home or an exchange, and Franklin and other explorers took from here their Canadian guides.

A great *Ononthio* has also now taken up his abode at La Chine, namely, Sir George Simpson, the Governor-General of the Hudson's Bay countries, so that one may say that the affairs of almost one-half of North America are conducted from this village.

The Hudson's Bay Company has indeed now only a few establishments or forts on the upper Ottawa, and the quantity of fur or other produce of the chase now brought here is very inconsiderable; for the whole produce of the country round Lake Superior is not as might be expected brought down the St. Lawrence or the Ottawa, but is mostly taken to Moose Factory and other ports on Hudson's Bay; and it has been so arranged because the goods can in this way, though by a great circuit, be shipped at once on the Company's own vessels, which assemble at certain times of the year in Hudson's Bay. It is probably not worth their while to send a ship to the St. Lawrence for the small quantity of fur it now yields.

It has been arranged, I am told, that the Governor of the Company's gigantic territory should reside at a point so far from the central places of their trade in those territories, because he is there nearer to Europe, and midway between England and most of the Hudson's Bay country; from there he can communicate quickly with Europe, and send his own or the Company's orders to the various forts and stations. The former French and English governors, who lived near Hudson's Bay, were cut off from Europe for eight or nine months in the year.

The renowned and highly respected Sir George Simpson has been himself a promoter of most of the modern Arctic voyages of discovery, and as he has also made a voyage round the world, and published an interesting account of it with which I was well acquainted, I took the liberty of waiting on him. His residence, Hudson's Bay House, as it is called, is a small and modest abode, strikingly contrasting with the palace of another Governor-General of an English land-owning company in the East, and I was interested in its details, the reception-rooms, the rooms of business, the courts for the fur magazines, and canoe-houses, probably because (*detractis detrahendis*) they afforded me an idea of the arrangement of " Cumberland House," " York House," and the other numerous Houses, which the Hudon's Bay Company have scattered over the whole of North-Western America, and where their sub-governors' chief traders and agents reside.

In the canoe-houses of La Chine I found a whole

fleet of quite new birch bark canoes, and was able to study the structure of this remarkable vehicle. A traveller of the north-west might well devote to them a whole chapter, as one in Arabia might to the camel, for without these birch bark canoes those wide regions would have been neither discovered nor turned to use. Birch bark is an extremely light material, and a canoe that will hold twenty men only weighs a few hundred-weight, and can be carried by three or four men, and is so elastic, that it more often yields than breaks when it receives violent blows among the rocks and cataracts. It is thoroughly soaked in oil that it may not imbibe water, and it is extremely easy to repair. The holes are sewed up with wire, you may darn it like a stocking, and patch it like a shoe, and stop up every little chink and opening in the most easy and expeditious manner. Only with such craft as this could it have been possible to navigate the labyrinth of streams in the north-west of America, where all the rivers are interrupted by innumerable cataracts and rapids, and a vessel meets with rough treatment at every step, and where a boat has to be drawn out of the water and carried several times in one day.

These canoes look something like long sausages, as they have no keel, and the ribs are bent in a circular form as affording a better resistance. Their lading and ballast must therefore always be carefully distributed and balanced, or they will roll over in the water like a round trunk of a tree. The ribs and timber are of course as narrow and thin as possible.

Sir George Simpson had on his table a small silver model of a canoe, in which every part was made of the precious metal, and this was certainly an appropriate place for so pretty a symbol of the whole floating traffic of the American north.

A steamer carried us from La Chine, first on the broad bosom of the Lake of St Louis, which consists still entirely of the greenish water of the St Lawrence. The brown-coloured Ottawa rolls the greater part of its waters through a long channel to the north of the Montreal island, and this is indeed recognised as its mouth by Canadian geographers. The great and fertile island of Montreal may indeed be regarded as the product of the confluence of these two streams. Its flat fields have certainly been often inundated by them, and covered with rich mud. They are as fruitful as a Delta country, and as the island is in a geological point of view, so is the city of Montreal in a political and economical one also, the product of their union.

From the Lake of St Louis, the steamer slipped

through a narrow pass and a group of islands into another lake. It is rather remarkable that this mighty St Lawrence has not yet worn down the rocky steps over which it flows, and hollowed out its rocky passes into a regular channel, but consists, like all the other rivers of the northern half of North America, of an endless chain of lakes, cataracts, rapids, and river-straits or narrows. In the Mississippi territory and the Alleghanies the character of the rivers is quite changed.

When we got higher up the lake near the termination of the island of Montreal we saw the two streams, the brown or red-brown Ottawa and the greenish St Lawrence, flowing by the side of each other. At first sight one is inclined to prefer the lighter coloured water to the dark fluid that almost looks as if it came out of a tan-yard, but in Montreal it has been decided that the Ottawa water is the better. The St Lawrence contains particles of lime and various salts in solution, and is therefore less available for domestic and culinary purposes; but the Ottawa has nothing of this kind, and receives its colour probably from plants which nevertheless do not affect its taste. In a glass its water is as clear as crystal, and it has therefore been determined to feed the new water-works of Montreal from the Ottawa instead of the St Lawrence. One becomes at last indeed reconciled even to the colour of the latter; it sometimes looks like melted amber, or a stream of pure coffee, and in' the whirlpools and cataracts, the dark brown masses of water make a new and pleasing contrast with the snow-white foam.

A great raft of wood was floating over the lake down the Ottawa, which is the chief forest plank and beam river in Canada, and supplies most of the timber for the trade of Quebec. On account of the manifold difficulties of the navigation, these rafts cannot be constructed like ours on the Rhine and Danube. They consist of a number of small rafts called cribs, which on broad lakes or tranquil parts of rivers move altogether; but where cataracts and rapids interrupt the navigation, they are divided, according to circumstances, into halves, sixths, or even their smallest constituent parts, cribs, and a few bold canoe-men seat themselves upon them and shoot with them down through the open channels into the fall. Below it the various members of the raft are collected again, and they then glide all together smoothly down to the next cataract, where they have to be taken to pieces again. The pilots or raftsmen are a strong and hardy class, and display a great amount of courage and contempt of death. Most of them are French-

Canadians, as they seem to understand the business best, and are the teachers of the Scotch and Irish, who come into the country as novices. They are nevertheless apt scholars, and occasionally surpass their teachers in boldness and skill. I was assured by a person well acquainted with these things, that in critical cases, when the Canadian himself loses courage, the appeal will be made successfully to a Briton who has not been two years on the Ottawa.

There are now above a dozen larger or smaller steamers on the Ottawa, but they navigate it only in a fragmentary manner. Between every two cataracts are stationed a few of these boats, which carry you over the lake or smooth part of the river, but you then go ten or twelve miles by land, till you come again to smooth water and more steamers, and the higher you go up the river the smaller they become. Our present one was as large and as luxuriously fitted up as the river steamers of America mostly are. The tables were covered at the appointed hours with a superabundance of all kinds of viands, and handsome and convenient little rooms were provided for our repose at night. I could not help thinking as we glided along in this floating palace, of the Jesuit fathers and their canoe voyages, and the numerous hardships and privations they underwent, and it was precisely on the river Ottawa that they made most of these adventurous journeys, of which they have left many descriptions. I had read them all, and at the sight of the shores and the thick woods, a hundred reminiscences came hovering before me, of the cataracts where Father A had lost his Bible and all his books; of the island where Father B, pursued by the Indians, had knelt down to pray, and so received his death-stroke; of the lakes along whose banks the Fathers C and D journeyed alone with their God among these wild men, to carry the tidings of the gospel to yet unknown regions; of the points and headlands where they had landed to cook their "Sagamité," or maize porridge, often the only food they tasted for long years, and over which they uttered their pious thanksgivings; of the hills on which they erected a wooden cross, or perhaps a little chapel, and collected the Indians around it to worship. How would they have rejoiced had they been able to see in prophetic vision their favourite river as it appears now, the towns arising out of its forests, the steamers foaming along its waters, the bridges spanning them from shore to shore.

The bridge beneath whose magnificent arches we passed out of the Lake of St Lawrence to that of the "Two Mountains," is a work worthy of the Romans. It is built of vast blocks of dark grey limestone, and has an aspect of solid grandeur worthy of its destination, namely, to form part of the Grand Trunk Railway, which is to connect the whole St Lawrence system from east to west. I wondered not a little to find so superb a work in so thinly inhabited a region; but here in Canada, as I have said, they build for the future, and on a grand scale; they give the child a wide garment, and leave it to grow up to it. There will soon be people enough to avail themselves of all these things.

Among the things that the Fathers would have rejoiced to see are also some neat, clean, and civilized Indian villages; but, unfortunately, there are not many of them, for civilization has acted on them rather as a destructive than as a regenerative force. The fragments of half a dozen tribes, which formerly wandered over wide regions, are now often collected in a single village, and gathered into one church. We saw an example of this near the bridge on the above-mentioned "Lake of the Two Mountains." It is the mission of the same name, and is inhabited by a few Algonquins, Iroquois, and others, but each of these fragments has a separate quarter of the village, and I was assured they never intermarry. Their language, at least those of the Algonquins and Iroquois, are as different as French and English, and though they have but one church, they have several priests, who preach to them in their own tongue. As we were approaching one of these Indian villages, I noticed a strikingly tall man who was preparing to leave the vessel. He was very well dressed, like a rather opulent farmer, and as I took him for a French Canadian, I addressed him in French. But he shook his head, "Not understand, *un petit brin Français.*" "Oh, you are an Englishman, are you?" said I. "I should not have thought so from your brown complexion and coal-black hair." But the head was shaken again—"Not understand, *aussi un petit brin Anglais.*"

"Ah, indeed! so you are German? Welcome, fellow-countryman; we can understand each other all the better." This I said in German, shaking my brown fellow-passenger's hand, and expected a genuine Black Forest or Harz Mountain salutation in return. But to my astonishment the stranger now looked completely puzzled, and remained dumb.

"Why, who in the world are you then, man?" said I, returning to my French—for I had never heard any other language in the country than these three.

"*I Savats,*" was the reply,—"*Iroka,*"—that is to say, I am a savage, or Iroquois.

I now looked more closely at him, and had no difficulty in recognising the serious and angular features of an Indian; and since he was much more accessible and courteous than many a European, who would have to look much higher up his genealogical tree for his anthropophagic ancestors, I had a very interesting conversation with him. We got on as well as we could with a little "bit of English" and a little "bit of French," and he told me that he came from a Canadian village many hundred miles to the west, and that he had journeyed hither to visit this Algonquin and Iroquois village, at the Lake of the Two Mountains, where he had some relations, and that he had also business to transact. He proposed to remain for the Sunday with his relatives, go to church with them, and return on the Monday.

When I questioned him concerning his sympathies towards the various European nationalities he answered: "Of all white what is—the Savats like Scotch most. Scotch most like the savages. Scotch language also like Savats, they say; but I speak them—I not understand." (The Scotch language is most like that of the savages; but though I speak to them, I do not understand them.)

It was rather curious to me, to see before me

a man as neat and well-dressed as any one of us, and whose agreeable, and even gentlemanly manner led you to infer a certain amount of inward culture, who yet did not hesitate to say —" I am a savage." I perceived that the word could not carry with it the *levis notæ macula* that it has with us; and the notion of the Iroquois that the Scotch were most like his countrymen, was at that time quite new to me. By degrees, however, I learned that that opinion is very widely diffused here, and the French Canadians, in order to distinguish the Highlanders from others, call them "*les Ecossais sauvages.*" The idea, too, that the language of the Scotch and Welsh is most like those of the Indians, is very prevalent. In the early times of American history, the people from Wales and Scotland used to say they recognised words of their own among the languages of the Indians of the South and West; and it was interesting to me to meet this idea again on the Ottawa. Whether it be in consequence of the real or supposed affinity that the Scotch have associated more intimately with the Indians than any other Britons, I know not; but it is a fact that the half-breeds in America, who are not the offspring of Frenchmen, are nearly all of Scotch descent — much less frequently of either English or Irish.

The Highlanders have not, indeed, much to complain of in being compared with the present Iroquois and Algonquins of Canada. To say nothing of the old barbarous system of Clanship, and of the Highland costume, which is exactly what would please an Indian chief, and of other things that might be mentioned, there is so much barbarism, poverty, dirt, and disorder to be found in the island and mountain villages of the Scotch highlands, that it would be a vast improvement, and a blessing for the country, if they could be raised to the level of the Iroquois villages of Canada, and exhibit the same amount of order, cleanliness, and humanity.

There are sometimes rich heiresses to be found among these savages, and to them the Britons do not fail to pay their court, as the young gentlemen in our German cities do to the daughters of wealthy peasants. On the "Lake of the Two Mountains" a handsome country-seat was pointed out to me, whose mistress, a squaw, or Indian woman, had brought her English husband a fortune of £20,000 sterling.

French *seigneuries* and French villages are still to be seen, though rather thinly scattered, for about 70 miles up the Ottawa, but beyond this all the settlements are new and British. The woods along the shores seemed endless, and now showed themselves in all the varied tints of their beautiful autumn foliage. Sometimes they and the hills whose sides they clothed, were interrupted by a valley and a river which flowed into the Ottawa,—and we mostly had a few passengers, or some chests and bales of goods, to send up each of these tributary streams. I inquired everywhere about the nature and aspect of the valleys and rivers towards the north, and I was told that at the mouths of these rivers there are often to be seen handsome European settlements, whilst their sources are still unknown, and are hidden somewhere in darkness and cold in the forests and mountains of Labrador.

One of these rivers, especially, is called "*La Rivière du Nord.*" Its course is so little known that it is drawn differently on every map; but at its mouth there already lies a town called St Andrew's, which has no fewer than six different churches, religions, and nations.

"Are there any Germans?" I asked of an inhabitant of this town, whom we had on board.

"Oh, yes, some," was the reply; "my wife is a German. The Germans are industrious people, and do very well. The richest man in our place is a German. We English call him *Allbrek*, but his real name is *Aollenbreekten* (Albrecht?). I wonder more Germans do not come. We have some French Canadians too in the town."

"How do you like them?" said I, for I was curious to know whether these people kept the same good name on the Ottawa that they have elsewhere.

"Oh, those Canadians, sir," replied the Englishman, "they are a fine, honest, mannerly set of people. It is true there are some among them like other people, but, upon the whole, the Canadians are most honest and *genteel*. There are neither liars, thieves, drunkards, nor blackguards among them. When I came here first, no Canadian would ever care to shut his door, and if you bought a cow or a piece of land from them they would never think about an oath or a paper. Since the revolution of 1837 the custom of shutting doors is become more general, but still their houses are always open for the poor and the stranger. If you ever, sir, have lost your way or feel tired, go to a Canadian house if you can find one, and you will see how they will receive you. They will make you as comfortable as they possibly can. That's what the Canadians are, sir."

CHAPTER XXI.

A PORTAGE.

The first division of our steam-boat journey carried us as far as a French place called Carillon, where we found a whole crowd of Canadian stage coaches with four horses, waiting to convey us further, but both the vehicles and the cattle had a very ancient and broken-down appearance.

As it rained and a very cold wind was blowing, the male part of the company were soon at the coach doors, and about to take the seats by storm, but at the door of each conveyance stood the coachman as sentinel, and placed himself and his whip unceremoniously across the entrance, and stopped the advancing tide, with "Halt, gentlemen! the ladies have not yet chosen their places!" and thereupon the masculine crowd drew back respectfully, and stood quietly in the rain till the ladies had slowly advanced, and placed themselves to their liking, and then the gentlemen slipped in and took what was left for them. I had myself, according to my custom, taken an outside place by the coachman without regard to the rain, and since it soon cleared up and the sun shone again, I could enjoy the prospect of the country as well as the conversation of my fellow-passengers. There were two of them, and the usual battery of questions soon began to play upon me. " Are you a stranger? Where do you come from? How long have you been in the country? How do you like the country? Where are you going to settle?" &c. And when I had answered all these inquiries punctually, one of my interrogators began again from the point of my country.

" You say you are a German?"

" Yes."

" Tell me, have you got an Established Church in Germany?"

" No."

" Have you both Protestants and Catholics?"

" Both."

" Have you most Protestants or Catholics?"

" I think the two parties must be pretty equally balanced."

" How many are there on each side?"

"I think perhaps sixteen or seventeen millions."

"Seventeen millions! By Jesus, there would be a famous battle if they were going to fight one another."

"Yes," said the other, "and what a profitable job it would be to furnish the *shillelahs*."

So without my asking any questions, I saw that I had by me a genuine son of Erin, and a regular Yankee. Only an Irish fancy would so instantly have boded forth a fight as the consequence of having seventeen millions of Protestants and Catholics "on each side;" and only Yankee associations have suggested immediately how to make a profit out of it.

The roads along which we drove were much more primitive than our carriages, and it required all the skill of a Canadian coachman, and all his practice in bad roads, to carry us pretty quickly, and in a good state of preservation, through all the holes and quagmires, and over all the blocks of stone and stumps of trees, that lay in our way.

The Canadian horse seems, in the course of centuries, to have acquired excellent qualities for this purpose. It is a most patient, persevering, indefatigable animal, and when I saw these courageous, willing, and much-harassed creatures, toiling over rocks and through morasses, I was often reminded of the almost indestructible horses of Poland and Russia.

"You are right," said the coachman; "our Canadian horses are the best for hardship and hunger, and very easy to feed. They are next to the mule for this." They resemble a good deal their Canadian peasant masters, I think, as indeed domesticated animals generally reflect many of the qualities of those who have trained them.

"The American horse is different," continued our driver; "it can't bear half as much, and wants better food and more care, but it is very light on the feet, and runs without a heavy load a great distance;" and thereupon he went into many minute details, and gave me more information than I am able to repeat; but, as I listened to him, it sometimes seemed to me as if he were describing the biped rather than the quadruped inhabitants of these regions.

The Canadian horses are said to be chiefly of the Norman race. They are spread through the whole St Lawrence territory, and still further to the West; they are much sought for their excellent qualities, and are sent to the Southern States, even as far as Virginia, and I afterwards saw many of them in Pennsylvania. The Canadian is one of the most strongly characterised and most widely diffused races of horses in America, and is only excelled by the Spanish horse which has reached the North by the way of Mexico.

These Spanish or Mexican horses may be said to have conquered the whole wide prairie lands towards the North, where they have multiplied so surprisingly, and have taken possession of the great pastures, north-west of Lake Superior, before one of their white masters could get so far. Such a wide distribution and return to a wild state has not taken place with the French Canadian horses, and no wild Indian tribe has been mounted by means of them, and the cause of the difference is, doubtless, the character of the country and the system of rivers, amongst which the French settled, and which made the ship and the canoe more necessary than the horse. All the French travels and excursions in Canada were foot journeys, whilst all the excursions and expeditions into the interior were equestrian.

The country through which we were travelling was almost as primeval in its aspect as the road. The ground on each side was covered by masses of rock and boulderstones, and fragments of limestone, gneiss, granite, and slate were as thick as tombstones in a church-yard; indeed they made the whole country look like a church-yard, and the same appearance was presented in various regions of the Ottawa, namely, at the portages, where the river has had to break through a rocky dam. Far in the interior of Canada and Labrador, too, these church-yard landscapes are said to be quite common.

I could hardly understand how it was worth any one's trouble to settle and cultivate the soil here, and yet all these stone-bearing fields were carefully hedged in with trunks of trees. " Why, sir, from amongst all these lumps of rock comes some of our finest and fattest beef," said my neighbours. " Look at that ox there, look at his ribs, look at his flanks, look at his broad chine; he don't look starved, does he? These stones that annoy you are particularly good for our meadows. In the spring the first tender young grass shoots up about their edges, and in the summer these stones retain the moisture, and nourish fresh grass, when the meadows without stones are all withered up, and now in the late autumn they keep it longer than it stays anywhere else. Just compare that stoneless spot there where all the plants have been long dead, with these block meadows, where the beasts still get plenty to eat;" and I was obliged to confess that in regions where the artificial irrigation of meadows is unknown, there may be some advantage in blocks. Some of the fields where it has been desired to raise crops of corn, have been cleared with spade and pick-axe, and gunpowder, but it must be a colossal undertaking, and I can easily imagine that our German emigrants, when they hear of the clean, rich, and stoneless lands of Iowa and Minnesota, are much inclined to pass by the mouth of the Ottawa.

The Ottawa has nevertheless a right to complain that the German immigrants have bestowed so little attention on this country. There is seldom more than one, or perhaps two Germans in a village; and even in the capital, Bytown, now called Ottawa, there are only some half dozen, who appear to have been flung there by chance. The great emigrant march goes straight to "the West," where alone success and fortune seem to beckon.

The Ottawa country is hardly known even by name to the Germans, and yet it seems to open a wide field for their industry, and offers many advantages besides these rock meadows, which, when the stones are once removed, yield very good crops.

Fine level fertile islands, with extremely rich soil, are common in the valley of the Ottawa. They are often large, and resemble in their main features the island of Montreal, and the Isle of Orleans at Quebec, which are renowned for their productiveness.

The demand for labour is as great here as anywhere in America. " Wanted 500 labourers to work on a canal in the Upper Ottawa; wages, $1\frac{1}{4}$ dollar a day, and lodging." " Wanted, 300 labourers to work on a Bridge," &c. on similar conditions. Announcements of this kind met the eye everywhere, and in Bytown, the capital of Ottawa, you could not look into a tailor's, shoemaker's, or any other shop without seeing a bill in the window notifying " the want of five or six workmen." Among the raftsmen, pilots, foresters, and wood-cutters of the Ottawa, there are no Germans to be found; and yet our country could furnish so many individuals well practised in these occupations. Can our men not maintain the competition with these strong and hardy races, or have our Black Forest raftsmen and wood-cutters still enough to do at home ? It cannot be the climate that keeps Germans from Ottawa. It is rough and cold indeed, but, as every one admits, incomparably more healthy than the valleys of the Mississippi and the Missouri.

" I 'll tell you what it is that frightens our countrymen away from the Ottawa, and from all Canada," said a German colonist of the Ottawa to me. " It is Queen Victoria of England ! I have often puzzled myself, as you are doing, to make out why there should be, by the latest census, only 15,000 Germans settled in Canada, when as many as that pass through the country every year."

"I have talked with a good many of them when I went down the St Lawrence, and recommended them to stay with us, but they almost all gave me the same answer, 'No, we did not come to America to be again the subjects of a crown. We have had enough of princes in our own country, and we left Europe to become free republican citizens.' It is their rooted prejudice against monarchy that makes the Germans pass, and indeed fly through this country. They do not know that the monarchy is with us merely a name, that we are as free and as self-governing as the Americans themselves, and have fewer taxes. Do, when you go home, tell our countrymen that they cannot live more freely anywhere in the whole world than they can here on the Ottawa. But they will soon find it out themselves, and then the stream of emigration will flow towards our country, but whoever comes first will be first served."

The conviction that the emigrants would soon arrive in crowds, and that the young Ottawa country is destined before long to play a great part, was one I found very generally diffused here. Probably these anticipations are chiefly founded on the present great extension of railways. The roads have been hitherto as rugged and as expensive as the one above described, and now we saw a locomotive rushing through the forest, and whistling among the labyrinth of rocks and boulders. It was making a trial trip on a piece of the Ottawa line that had been just finished, and which was to be opened in a few days, so the dragging of canoes in the old Jesuits' fashion, and the stage-coach torture, may be considered to be all over at this portage.

"But can such a costly undertaking as a railroad possibly pay in a still unpeopled country?" The question showed that I came from Germany, where a new road is seldom opened till a number of passengers are standing waiting for it, and where nobody makes a railroad on speculation.

"We hope and expect that the railroad will bring us the passengers and the population it is intended to carry," was the reply. "They will come, though we do not yet know where from nor how. They will shoot up like weeds out of the ground when the railroad has touched and fertilized it. Railroads with us are magic wands, horns of plenty, from which we scatter the seeds of a population, and they spring up and fill the place we have made for them as water does when you dig a canal in a moist country."

As the faith in the magic power of railways is one very generally held here, people are very willing to assist in their construction. An opulent landowner, who was one of my travelling companions, informed me that many farmers along the whole line had hastened to offer the Company all the land they required without any compensation. His own estate, he said, was cut into two halves by this line, but the only remuneration he had asked was that the Company would make him a tunnel under the line to connect them. This would afford him a most ample compensation, besides the advantage of the line itself, for the people here are as eager to get a line running over their land as in a desert they might be to get a canal.

It may easily be supposed that the prevalence of such views diminishes very much the expenses of railroads; and also that the Railway Companies, being generally encouraged and supported in this way, make short work with the obstinate individuals they occasionally meet with. We noticed an example of this as we went along. The line at one point passed right across a place where a farmer had begun to build himself a large barn, and as he had demanded a very large compensation, the impatient Railway Company, without further ceremony, sent a number of men armed with saws and axes, to pull down the buildings, and throw the great beams and other building materials on each side on the farmer's land, leaving him to go to law if he thought proper. But if the powerful companies are sometimes thus despotic in their proceedings, private individuals are also violent, revengeful, and inconceivably reckless. A case of this kind appeared lately in the papers, of a farmer, who, not having received what he thought adequate compensation, did everything in his power to obstruct the line where it passed over his land, and when he could not succeed, at last hit on a truly infernal project. He built one night a kind of hut or scaffolding across the rails, placed a barrel of gunpowder inside it, and planted himself in readiness with a match. In the morning when the train came up the engine-driver fortunately discovered the contrivance in time, and stopped to parley. The man declared the land was his, and he had a right to order off any one he pleased, and that if the train dared to approach, he would blow it up and himself with the rest. There was a long delay and a great many contrivances to get hold of the madman, and at last his antagonists succeeded in engaging him in negotiation, while some of the men crept round unperceived, got possession of the powder, and disarmed him.

Carillon, which lies at the beginning of our twelve-miles-broad isthmus, is the last French village. All beyond this are new British settlements, filled with Irish, Scotch, &c., and they do not wear by any means so pleasing an aspect as the old French ones. The first of these is Grenville, the opposite pole of the Portage; but it consists merely of wooden log-houses, among the rocks and tree stumps. The place seems, however, to be well provided with churches; indeed, to have nearly as many as houses. There was a little Presbyterian Church of stone, with two windows; an English High Church with three; a Methodist Chapel, built of wood, and not larger than a log hut; and a Catholic Church, with a cross made of two laths nailed together, and probably quite after the model of the first chapels that the Jesuits erected in the country.

From Grenville, where by degrees all the four-horse coaches came in, we glided like swans down a beautiful smooth part of the Ottawa river, which here again assumes a majestic appearance, consisting of a long broad expanse of water, like a rapidly flowing lake, bordered on either side with wooded hills.

Several of these straight, regularly formed portions occur as exceptions to the usually winding and irregular course of the Ottawa, but the most remarkable is that which is found about the middle of its course, above Bytown, and which bears a special name among the Canadians, though I have unluckily forgotten it. At this part of the river the current seems to have cut through the rocks, like a cannon-ball, and formed a broad channel of from 30 to 40 miles in length, between high perpendicular walls of stone. You can look through it with a glass, from one end to the other; the depth of water is everywhere equal, and it flows quite smoothly. Canal digging would be most superfluous if Nature had formed rivers in general like this part of the Ottawa.

A section of somewhat similar character had occurred at Grenville, and our steamer glided pleasantly over its brown, glassy surface. The mountains were here higher and grander than further down the river, and not entirely uninhabited. As it grew dark we could see lights twinkling here and there out of the woods, occasionally showing faint outlines of windows and houses, and as Carillon was the last village, we here reached the last " *Seigneurie de la petite nation,*" as it was called. Here dwells, in complete retirement, M. Papineau, whose name was so conspicuous in the Revolution of 1837, and who has been called the Mirabeau of Canada;

but I only saw his habitation from afar, as circumstances unfortunately did not permit of my paying him a visit.

Saw-mills, and board and plank cutting establishments, little harbours and bays filled with rafts of the rudest construction, made of colossal trunks of trees, and ballasted with lumps of rock, piers or bridges for landing,—these were the chief features of this portion of the river, as of the former. These piers often issue straight from the forest into the river, without any road or even any habitation being discoverable near them, and yet there must be such in the interior, for small one-horse carts were tied under the trees, in readiness to receive the goods,—sacks of salt, chests, and bales of cottons, axes, spades, pick-axes, &c., which we had brought, and which we piled up as quickly as possible on the piers. Where all that was to go to, and who was to use it, remained a mystery hidden in the forest; but it was evident that here, where I often thought myself on the very outermost limits of civilization, there were, as our German proverb says, "More people living behind the hills."

We brought, to my surprise, very few living creatures up the river with us, and a single sheep, with long fleece, constituted, I believe, the whole of our live cargo; and, consequently, the poor animal had an immense amount of criticism and complimenting to undergo. He was tied up at the fore-part of the vessel, and formed, during the whole Ottawa journey, a central point of interest for the passengers, who gathered round him smoking and gossiping, and since they had nothing else to do, examining his wool, and his teeth, and his flesh and fat, and making him the subject of everlasting discussions. Every ten minutes came up a few more gentlemen who had just finished their cigars, and did not know what to be at: and then down they sat by the poor bleating sheep, and began pulling and feeling, and poking him about, and instituting, like their predecessors, curious inquiries into the character of his wool, fat, &c. If ever a sheep was thoroughly investigated, it was that one, and I was quite glad when I at last heard his bleating from one of the pier-heads, and knew that he had reached the place of his destination, and that for the time his troubles were over.

So were not ours, as yet, for about midnight we landed on a high shore, where the navigation of the river terminates, and had then half an hour's race over marsh and corderoy roads, before we found ourselves safely lodged in the capital, Bytown, in one of the large crowded hotels, of which, in the youngest towns of Canada, there is never any lack.

CHAPTER XXII.

BYTOWN OR OTTAWA.

It is little more than 25 years since the first tree was felled on the spot where now stands Bytown, and it is a very few years since there existed here anything that could be called a town, and yet it already covers as much ground as Boston, and though its inhabitants did not, when I visited it, exceed 10,000, it was as grand in its pretensions as Quebec or Montreal. As yet it was only called a *town*, but as soon as its inhabitants should exceed the number above mentioned, it was to be declared a city, and, as a corporation, would attain to a greater amount of independence, and it was proposed that its name should then be altered. Its present one is taken from that of a Colonel By, and signifies merely By's Town; but it awakens an association of ideas, by which the vanity of the citizens is not flattered, for whoever is unacquainted with the historical derivation of the name considers it equivalent to "Out-of-the-way Place," and this the Bytowners do not at all approve of. Half a dozen other names have been proposed, and amongst them that of Ottawa City, which has been adopted as well sounding and significant of its situation and dignity as the metropolis of the young Ottawa country. Other Canadian settlements have changed their names when they rose to the civic rank, as, for instance, Toronto, which was before called York.

The first occasion of building a town here was this. Both shores of the St Lawrence are Canadian, or British, as far up as a little way above the mouth of the Ottawa, but from that point the southern one begins to be American; and since this part of the river is also difficult to navigate on account of the number of cataracts, the British Government was desirous of finding a more inland water-communication between East and West Canada, by which the transport of troops, or other operations, could be undertaken without disturbance or observation from the Americans. They therefore passed up the Ottawa as far as its confluence with the Rideau, a small river which, by means of a series of lakes, has a pretty direct communication with the important town and fortress of Kingston on Lake Ontario; and it was determined to perfect the communication by canalling, and so obtain a much safer and more convenient route for soldiers and munitions of war than that of the St Lawrence. Colonel By, of the Engineers, was commissioned to undertake the work, and this was the origin of the Rideau Canal, and thence also arose in the midst of the forest, at the mouth of the Rideau, where the chief supplies were received in the Ottawa, a little settlement of labourers, boatmen, engineers, &c.; and since in Canada you cannot drop a spark but that forthwith arises a forest conflagration, so from this little collection of huts sprang up the present city with its numerous houses, shops, magazines, churches, schools, colleges, and other buildings, varying in size and style, that now cover so wide an extent of ground. The man who gave his name to the city is still living in the "Old Country;" nay, the woodman who cut down the first tree, and the stone-mason who hewed out the first block of stone for its foundations, are still extant, and their fortunes have run parallel with those of the city. They are rich land-owners, "Honourables, and Senators;" but the town still bears traces of its recent forest-birth, and presents a singular aspect.

There has been as yet no time to pave the streets, and in bad weather they are in a desperate state; only near the houses, as in most of the youngest towns of Canada, there run what are called "plank-roads," that is, footpaths made of boards. As for gardens, fruit-trees, or flowers, no one has had time so much as to think of them, and the old rough boulders and masses of rock are lying about still among the groups of houses, and firs and other forest trees are springing up again out of the stumps. Here and there amongst elegant colleges and churches are to be seen fragments of the primeval forest, lofty pines and firs, and thick underwood that occasionally may give shelter to a bear. Many spots still covered with these moss-grown rocks, roots, and stumps, are nevertheless enclosed, and serve sometimes for keeping cattle. By and by they will be changed into gardens, but as yet the unbroken mass of the primeval forest fences in the town on all sides, up to its very streets, and if you get a view of it from a high point you see for miles and miles nothing but a sea of woods, in which the town lies like the nest of a heathcock.

The grand pretensions of Bytown tend to nothing less than to be made the seat of Government and Parliament, and the residence of the Governor-General of all Canada, an honour for which no less than four cities have been contending.

Quebec first put in its claim, on account of its position nearest the mouth of the St Lawrence, and its being the political centre of this great empire. According to the letter of the law hitherto, Quebec on the east, and Toronto on the west, were to share the honour between them, and each city receive the preference every four years. But this perpetual change is found, as may be supposed, very inconvenient, and the Quebec people think that as the Government is now in their city, it ought to remain there.

Montreal, the largest and most populous town in the country, the centre of its commerce, and the most like a metropolis in appearance, was for a long time the seat of Government, but in a popular insurrection the Government buildings and Parliament houses were burnt, and the authorities left the place. Montreal hopes nevertheless to be restored to its former dignity.

Toronto, the capital of the whole British West, which looks on Lower Canada as a very antiquated, unprogressive, and half Frenchified country, desires to remove the Parliament and the seat of Government quite out of the influence of the French atmosphere of Quebec, and to have it established in the centre of the hopeful rapidly advancing western country; and Toronto has so little doubt of its success, that the sites for the Government buildings are already pointed out.

At last comes Bytown, a city of scarcely more than twenty years of age, throwing its sword into the scale, and maintaining its claim to the character of a metropolis. At first I was rather astounded at this pretension, but on further consideration it did not appear to me altogether unfounded. In the first place, as the Bytowners have calculated, their city has geographically the most central position in all Canada, and is, on the average, nearer to the most important places in the country than Quebec, Toronto, or even Montreal, and so many telegraph lines, canals, and railroads are making, or made, that Bytown is already intimately interwoven with the whole network by which the traffic of Canada is carried on. The persons forming and connected with the Government who would have to reside here, and who are accustomed to the enjoyments and luxuries of civilization, would find indeed no theatres, concert-rooms, &c., but what is there that cannot be quickly procured in America; and, on the other hand, they would not find here violent party discord among the inhabitants, and an unruly mob, such as that which burnt the Parliament Houses in Montreal. In the United States it is an old and judicious custom to place the centres of

Government out of the more populous towns, in comparatively *by-places*, where it can act with less fear of disturbance and better provide for the welfare of the country. The relation of Bytown to Montreal is in this point of view the same as that of Albany to New York.

Finally, Bytown has the advantage, at least over Montreal and Toronto, of being more secure from attack by an external enemy. Each is nearer to the frontier than Bytown, and cannot be made so secure in a military point of view; they are more exposed to *coups de main*. Bytown lies more in the interior—has an excellent natural site for an Acropolis and citadel, and its enabling military preparations to be carried on without approaching the frontier, was, as I said, the very occasion of its origin. The rivalry between the three large cities of Canada is also in favour of the claims of the future Ottawa city, and, it is said, it really has the best chance, so that the matter is very likely to end like the Presidential Elections in the United States, where the mutual jealousies of the powerful parties have the effect of keeping a Webster, Scott, or Clay out of the chair, and raising to it a Filmore and other inferior men.

CHAPTER XXIII.

THE FALLS OF THE OTTAWA.

THE most remarkable feature of Nature in the neighbourhood of Ottawa is the renowned cataract, called by the Jesuits, its discoverers, "*La Chaudière,*" or "Kettle Fall," and it is this which has fixed the town precisely on the spot which it occupies, and made some of its arrangements possible and others necessary.

There occurs here one of the most considerable joints or knots of the Ottawa river, a sudden deep depression, hollow, or cauldron, into which fall from lofty, rocky banks, three separate rivers ; first, the Ottawa, in its far-stretched fall, the *Chaudière;* secondly, the *Rideau,* or Curtain, so named from its falling in a veil-like sheet or curtain from a rocky ledge ; and thirdly, from the north, the *Gatineau,* which also has its cataracts and *Salto-mortale.*

The whole mass of the water of the Ottawa

throws itself over a rocky precipice along a line of half a mile in length, and the scenery is in many respects worthy a comparison with Niagara,—the height of the fall is indeed much less, but the volume of water is, at least at times, fully equal.

It has been calculated that at Niagara 500,000 tons shoot down the fall every minute, and this quantity remains pretty much the same all the year through, as the lakes by which it is fed undergo little change; but the Ottawa is very variable, having high water in the spring, and low in autumn; the average quantity however is, according to calculation, equal to that of Niagara—namely, 500,000 tons a minute.

The cataract lies immediately above, almost in the town, and a fine suspension bridge crosses the river from shore to shore, in full sight of the foaming fall, and affords a superb view of it. The rocky cliff forms here a many-curved line, with numerous projections and indentations, and a number of flat table-rocks that break the line. The water was so low when I reached it, that it could not be called one fall; there were a hundred streams falling in separate niches, and this circumstance gives an original character to the Chaudière. Many of its divisions form separate scenes, like a drama in five acts, and the fate of these separate streams is afterwards very various. Some of them are turned off artificially, and used to drive saw-mills and other works; one falls into a quite separate rocky bottom, where it whirls round for a while and then disappears in the earth, and it has not yet been discovered where it goes to, or where it returns to the light of day.

As in the Horse-shoe Fall at Niagara, there is here a place where the falling mass has worn away the rock more than elsewhere, where the cliff retires farthest back, and the greater part of the river throws itself over a single point; but this great scene is, alas, also the most inaccessible, as it often happens that the true kernel of a matter is hard to get at. This is the spot that really looks like a cauldron, and from which the whole receives its name. The clear brown floods come rushing in here from all sides, as if poured out of so many urns, into one and the same hole, and the dark transparent outpourings look like dark columns in a snow-storm. Out of the very centre of these rises a black table-rock, which alone would give a most picturesque effect to the scene, but that unluckily, as I have said, you cannot get near enough to obtain a proper point of view. Above, at the real beginning of the fall, were sticking in among the rocks some half-decayed timbers from a raft that made shipwreck here and could not be got out again.

If you leave the suspension bridge and proceed along the thickly-wooded banks of the river, you get from various points surprising views of the whole scene.

What an ancestor for a future great and wealthy family might some one of those old Canadian *Seigneurs* have become, if he had got possession in time of this picturesque and powerful fall. He might now have disposed of all manner of "water privileges," at what prices he pleased; but these old *Seigneurs* who halted near the *Petite Nation* dreamed not of a Bytown and Ottawa metropolis.

The ingenious arrangements for turning off and employing separate streams of water for the various machinery of the works, now springing up in such numbers round the falls, contributes not a little to enhance the interest of the locality.

Formerly the great masses of timber which came down the Ottawa were sent on in their rough state to Quebec, and there cut up into planks, and otherwise prepared for shipment to Europe. But since the rise of Bytown this work has been mostly performed on the spot, and the trunks of trees have been cut up directly into the required forms at sawing and planing mills, and so a considerable saving in transport is effected.

American immigrants from New England have

given the first impulse to these undertakings, and, indeed, you find them everywhere in Canada, where there is anything new going on. Like· the wild swans or swallows of the spring, they precede the advancing tide of culture and colonization, and if you miss them at Montreal, Quebec, and other old towns, you are certain to find them at places which, like Bytown, have just sprung into life. These Yankees have lately discovered iron in this country, and have set to working the mines; and to them also belong the most important saw-mill and wood-working establishments.

It is a real pleasure to go over such a well-managed place, for the Americans in all their arrangements do not merely attend to order and convenience, but also to agreeableness and elegance. They have introduced ornament and luxury even into a saw-mill. Their machines are so beautifully made, that they are quite pretty to look at, and the cutting part of them, the chisels, the planes, the saws, glitter like the finest steel. At other parts the dark colour of the iron is relieved by a streak of red or blue paint. The apartments are all spacious and convenient, and air, light, and water are distributed everywhere in abundance.

The thing that surprised me most, however, was the dwelling-house which the American owners of these mills have fitted up for their workmen. It is a most agreeable-looking boarding-house of quite elegant architecture, and the interior is equal in cleanliness to the quarter-deck of an English man-of-war. The workmen have their common breakfast and dining-rooms, as in the hotels of New York and Boston, and in their sleeping-rooms the most exact regulations were laid down for the linen and other things supplied to them. I must confess I delight in a country where wood-cutters and workmen at a saw-mill can command such an amount of comfort and decorum in their mode o life. Perhaps the Americans had in this case been desirous of showing the " Britishers " how such an establishment ought to be managed.

I found here at Bytown at last the original of an interesting picture I have seen somewhere, but I cannot now tell where, of the remarkable works and scenery of the sluices of the Rideau Canal. I have said that the Rideau river falls from a very high rocky plateau into the Ottawa, and a whole chain of locks one above another has therefore been found necessary in making the canal. They form together a sort of water stair-case, on which a vessel is raised up step by step, and which resemble together the renowned sluice-works of the Trolhatta Canal in Sweden. It is a scene deserving a better picture than the one I remember, and if a German landscape-painter should ever extend his excursions so far, he would find subjects that would rejoice both himself and the civilised world.

CHAPTER XXIV.

THE LUMBER-MEN.

DURING the day a respected inhabitant of Bytown had been showing me about and entertaining me in the most hospitable manner, and in the evening he delivered me to a friend not less complaisant. I passed it with a gentleman, who as Crown Timber Agent has under his inspection not less than sixty thousand square miles of forest land, the whole wood and forest district of Ottawa. He had a large map of this district, with all its rivers and forests, hanging up in his office, and the Scotch and Irish lumber-men who desire to undertake a piece of forest come to him, and have pointed out to them the portion on the map, on this or that creek or lake, for which they desire to be licensed, and for which they then pay their entrance tax.

A considerable attack has been made on the forest, on the Ottawa, to the distance of about 150 miles above Bytown, but beyond this there are immense thickly wooded tracts that have scarcely been touched by the axe. There is work and the reward of work for at least four hundred years to come, without counting what might in the mean while spring up again in the districts cut down. This has been pretty closely calculated. Below Bytown, near the river, the primeval forest has been mostly cut down, and only here and there do you see some giant fragments of the old world rising up out of the newer bush. Even in those tracts, however, which may be regarded in some measure as used up, new discoveries are continually made, or old treasures made more accessible. Every new canal or road, every attempt to render navigable a stream not before ventured on, leads to treasures of timber which had been passed by, because they could not be moved. In the woods of Ottawa it is as in mines, where old forsaken veins of metal, or gangways, that have been allowed to stand still, are opened again and carried into the interior of the mountain.

The lumber-men go spying about in all the side valleys and tributary streams of the Ottawa, to find out untouched pieces of forest, or the way to them.

and since all the woods belong, of course, not to the finder, but to the whole Province of Canada, it is then necessary for them to procure a licence, which they obtain for a certain yearly ground-rent per acre. They then begin to fell timber wherever they like, and pay, when they bring it to market, a duty of a half-penny the cubic foot, to the Provincial Government. They must, however, bring a certain quantity to market out of every acre of forest, and if they do not bring this minimum their ground-rent is doubled, or their licence withdrawn. By this system all interests are thought to be secured; the ground-rent is a kind of fee or entrance-money for the consolidation of the contract; the half-penny per cubic foot regulates the tax according to the better or worse harvest obtained, and the last-mentioned regulation prevents a rich capitalist from taking great tracts, and if it so please him leaving them unemployed, thereby raising the price of wood and injuring the revenue of the Government.

When people here speak of "lumber-men," they do not mean merely the labourers in the woods, but also the capitalists and speculators, the owners of saw-mills, and other great traders in timber. For example, the Gilmores of Glasgow, who have two hundred ships of their own on the St Lawrence and Ottawa, and possess numerous wood-cutting establishments about Bytown, are a family of "lumber-men."

Capitalists like these employ, at their own cost, great numbers of workmen, whom they send up the rivers into the woods, keeping them there winter and summer. These woodmen are known by their old French name of "*Gens de Chantier*," and the small log-houses that they build for dwellings in the forest are called *chantiers*—a word that the English have adopted, but corrupted into *shanty*, and in the same way they make shanty-men out of *Gens de Chantier*. The word has emigrated to the United States, where every poor hut or provisional dwelling is called a "shanty;" as, for instance, a squatter's shanty—but they talk sometimes of axe-men instead of shanty-men.

When a portion of forest has been marked out for cutting, a party of ten or twenty shanty-men is sent up to it, and they find out a spot where water and other advantages are to be obtained, and there set up their *chantier*, or log-house. In the Hudson's Bay Counties it would be called a "Fort." It is without windows, and a good deal like an Esquimaux hut. In the midst blazes a fire that is never let out, and the smoke passes out through a hole in the roof. The sleeping-places of the men are all round, as in the cabin of a ship. Other little huts are built for their stores, and the trunks of trees the men cut down piled up near them. In the winter these are dragged hither over the snow, and in the following spring sent down the water.

The axe-men are often of various nations, and since they have their log-houses far in the forests, hundreds of miles from civilization and the police, it occurred to me that the shanties might often be the scene of disorders and excesses; but I everywhere heard these woodmen praised for their order and sobriety. No robbery or crime, I was assured, is ever heard of among them, and in the midst of the axe-men of Labrador and Hudson's Bay, you would be safer than in the streets of New York. This, if true, is probably in some measure to be attributed to the good organization and distribution of the work, but also to the just and strict superintendence of the employers.

Every shanty has its Foreman, who assigns to each man his work, and also watches over his conduct. The French call him "*le Conducteur*," though sometimes also "le Foreman," and he makes his report at the end of the winter to the "*Boorshaw*." What kind of person a "Boorshaw" was, of whom I first heard from an English axe-man, I could not guess— but at length I made out that the word was an Anglification of *Bourgeois*, as the French *Gens de*

Chantier had been in the habit, from old times, of calling their employer or chief in the town.

"*Oui, oui, Monsieur, soyez sur le Foreman dans chaque chantier a son livre secret, dans lequel il note chaque manque de respect ou d'amitié, chaque effronterie ou combat, aussi chaque jour de maladie ou d' oisiveté. A la fin d' hiver il presente son livre au bourgeois, et le bourgeois est juste, mais sevère et sans pitié. Il ne paye que les jours où l' on travaille, et il degage de son service à l' instant les personnes desagréables.*

That these Foresters are, in general, so peaceful and "agréables" * is doubtless in a great measure attributable to the circumstance of their being, whether voluntarily or not, Temperance Men. Spirituous drinks never find their way to these remote shanties, and formerly the men drank only mock coffee made of toasted corn, but lately they have had real coffee and tea. Their principal food is salt meat and "*du loard*" (bacon). "*Oui, Monsieur, du loard c'est bon pour eux, ça leur donne beaucoup de force.* The only article of luxury or pleasure they are allowed is tobacco, though in the beginning of the spring, when the winter work is over and the snow not yet melted, they sometimes manage to get

* Agréables does not here mean pleasant, but peaceable. It is derived from *agrees*, to agree with.

a little sugar by tapping the maple trees and boiling down the juice.

"What do the men do on Sundays?" I asked. "Well, they mend their clothes and their tools, or lie upon their buffalo skins and smoke and talk."

"Have they no kind of religious instruction?" "No, none! unless perhaps the foreman reads to them a bit."

I wonder that no wandering preacher or Missionary has yet bethought himself of the case of these thousands of woodmen, hidden in hundreds of little settlements about the Ottawa forests, or endeavoured to bring them into the fold of the Church, and furnish them with some kind of spiritual food. They live as neglected in these respects as the herdsmen of the high Alps. But perhaps it is better so. It is better that the Catholic Irish and French, and the Protestant Scotch and English, should live thus as sheep without shepherds, but at peace with one another, than if the shepherds came and sowed discord among them.

The foremen of the shanties are usually Scotchmen, and indeed they are the leading men in all "lumbering" operations. They are not only the first men on the Exchanges of Quebec and Montreal, but the owners of most of the great timber establishments of Bytown, and the chiefs and leaders in the woods, and this may perhaps, in some measure, explain the good order that reigns in those remote regions.

The Scotch are a sober, thoughtful, calculating people, and make excellent advocates and judges; and they understand, too, how to bring men together, to guide them, and control their passions. The admirable system of government in the Hudson's Bay Territory is, I believe, mainly of Scotch invention, and all machinery is set in motion by Scottish heads and Scottish arms. They may be said to rule the whole of North America, and that without soldiers or armed force of any kind, but with a few hundred clever agents—" Traders " and " Chief Traders," for these are the modest titles taken by highly-respected and influential men, who, in Russia, would be called governors, or generals. Not by bayonets and cannon, but by wise policy, and just and strict administration, has this Hudson's Bay Company attained its almost irresistible power, which extends too over many different races of Indians. It settles their disputes, forbids their wars, determines the prices of their goods, and conducts all their business. Its information is so extensive and complete, that throughout North America not a skin can be sold without the Hudson's Bay Company being aware of the fact; and it maintains so jealously its privilege of exclusive dealing with the Indians, that no one can hope to interfere with it with impunity. Should, for instance, any speculator, thinking that the Company's territory is large, and its policemen and *gens d'armes* not very numerous, venture to enter their country without a passport, and try to trade on his own account with the Indians, it would go ill with him. If the Company should refuse him " fire and water," no Indian would venture to give him shelter or food, far less to trade with him. He would inevitably starve.

Here on the Upper Ottawa, indeed, the Company has no such exclusive privilege, although it does, *de facto*, rule and reign. On the second great secondary river, the Saguenay, the Company formerly farmed an extensive district from the Governor of Canada, and paid £1500 a year for the hunting, trading, and general utilizing of a tract as large as the kingdom of Saxony; but the lease has not lately been renewed, and the Company's exclusive privilege has ceased; and since then no fewer than 10,000 persons have emigrated and settled in the district.

It is probable that on the Ottawa, also, the Company will soon have to retire before the flood of immigration. " We look forward to the time," said a Canadian to me, when our towns and villages will reach to the shores of Hudson's Bay. Between the St Lawrence and James's Bay there is a great deal of good arable land, and that will some day form part of the great Canadian Empire.

CHAPTER XXV.

VISIT TO THE INDIANS IN THE FOREST.

THE quails of Canada are remarkably fine-flavoured, and no less so a certain kind of aromatic wild plum, indigenous to the country. They are found in the woods, and in the autumn are boiled and preserved with sugar in Canadian households, and then they may be presented by a fair hand to a friend who is to be hospitably entertained. On my expressing on such an occasion a wish to know more of a plum-tree that deserves to be renowned through the world, I was told by my host, "There grow plenty of them in a bit of forest belonging to me, a few miles off the town, and just now there is a party of Indians camping there, with my permission. If it were not so late we would walk out there this evening, and then you could make acquaintance with the plum-tree and the Indians at the same time."

My worthy host did not know what it was to give such a hint to me—and he had to pay the penalty. I begged him not to mind the lateness of the hour, and we were soon setting out armed with sticks and lanterns, to make a call on the Indians in the forest in this dark autumn night. On leaving the town we crossed a few fields, meadows, and enclosures, and soon came to the wood. It was a piece of the primeval forest, which seen by the light of our lanterns had a strange and picturesque effect. My friend carried his light round the thick trunks of some elms and maples, to enable me to judge of their girth, and we then looked up the long shafts, and saw their mighty boughs rising up into the starry sky.

It is remarkable what peculiar forms these Canadian trees assume. Elms and beeches and poplars all shoot up without a branch to an immense height, and then spread out into a leafy roof or cupola like palm trees. Oaks are, in our country, thick and gnarled, but here there are tall slender oaks. I saw many which, like pine-trees, could have been taken at once from the forest to serve as the masts of ships.

The part of the woods through which we were walking formed a rich and beautiful foreground, covered in the most wonderful manner with moss-grown stones, whole and half decayed trees, shrubs, weeds, and copses of the wild plum, and crossed by little brooks that we had to wade through. We were rather anxious to know whether we should find our Indians, for my friend had not seen them lately, and was not sure that they were not gone. But we soon perceived the glimmer of a distant light among the trees, and ascertained that this was from their watch-fire, which shone brighter and brighter as we advanced, and at last lit up a whole forest scene for us.

We advanced cautiously for fear of alarming the poor people, and found two women—an elder and a younger, mother and daughter, seated under a very airy kind of tent, which consisted, indeed, of nothing more than a large cloth spread over a few boughs of trees tied together. The elder woman was occupied in basket-making; the younger was stirring the fire, made of great branches and roots of trees, and both had their naked feet in the hot ashes, so that they seemed to me to be roasting. They remained quite undisturbed and busy at their work, and when we wished them good evening, answered our salutation very simply, without asking us any question about what we wanted or where we came from.

We expressed a hope that we had not frightened

them, and they said, No; they had heard us coming when we were a good way off. We sat down by the fire, and continued the conversation; but their answers were always shorter than our questions. We learned that they were Iroquois, from a village on the "Lake of the Two Mountains," that I had passed the day before. The men of the family, father and son-in-law, had gone further up the Ottawa to hunt, some months ago; the women had accompanied them as far as Bytown, and were waiting for them to return afterwards together to their village on the lake, and in the mean time were earning their living by basket-making. They worked in the evening and at night, and in the day-time the daughter carried their little manufactures to the town, and the mother took care of the tent, looked for berries, boiled maize, and got something for the daughter to eat on her return. The old woman spoke no word of English, but the daughter, who also understood a few words of French, made civil replies to our questions.

A hundred yards off there was another "camp," as it was called, though it consisted, like this, of only a single tent. To this, which was an Algonquin camp, we scrambled over the rocks and other natural barricades that had been left between the two. The occupants were precisely as in the tent of the Iroquois, an old and a young woman, but from certain whimpering sounds that proceeded from under a sheep-skin, we perceived that the younger woman had two children. Here also the elder matron was deaf and dumb to European language, and only the younger could speak a little broken French. While we were talking, the former sat still without granting us so much as a look, though her fingers continued in busy motion over the large basket that she had in hand; and the elastic strips of wood were pushed hither and thither, and the superfluous ends fell under her knife almost with the rapidity of an American steam saw-mill. We inquired, the daughter being interpreter, whether she would not now allow herself a little rest, as it was now ten o'clock; but she replied very briefly: "The baskets bring in very little. They must be ready to-morrow. We work every night." When we asked how old she was, the daughter's French arithmetic quite broke down. She could count as much as ten, but was puzzled how to express any higher number, and therefore explained to her mother in Algonquin what we wanted to know.

As soon as she had understood the question, the old lady laid aside her basket, spread out her ten fingers, and then struck her two hands at regular intervals seven times together; she then snatched her basket again, and went on plaiting as busily as before.

I could not get out of my head the picture of this grey-haired woman of seventy, sitting there on the bare damp ground in the comfortless forest, so hard at work; and I could not help thinking that the accusation of sloth, so commonly made against the poor Indians should be received " *cum grano salis.*"

Nearly eighty years ago, that is, about the year 1780, an Englishman, named Alexander Henry, travelled up the Ottawa, when as yet there was no thought of Bytown or of steam boats. His report, which was published in New York in 1809, contains a statement, which he had derived from his boatmen, that the Algonquin Indians of the lake of the Two Mountains claim the whole country on the Ottawa, as far as Lake Nipissing, as their property, and that it is regularly divided among them, a certain portion being assigned as hereditary in each family, and that they are very strict in the maintenance of these rights. "Any infringement of them is regarded as a gross insult, and the perpetrator worthy of death."

I should have liked to have translated this passage to the ancient Algonquin woman, and to have heard what she had to say on the subject. Very likely she was herself a great heiress, and regarded the whole Bytowners together as invaders and "worthy of death." These scanty relics of those who were once the lords of the soil do, it must be owned, profit too little by its present prosperity. They make a most melancholy impression, sitting there in some out-of-the-way corner in the woods, and seeing at a distance the towers of the invaders' city; and the great river, once their own, and traversed only by the canoes of their bold sons, ruled by the giant Steam. Truly may it be said to them in the words of the Bible, "I will cast thee out of the land of thy fathers, and thou shalt be a stranger in thine own land."

I could not help noticing how even these feeble remnants of tribes, almost entirely dispersed, still preserve the names, the languages, and the peculiarities of their forefathers, and the ancient enmities of their race still live in these atoms of the tribe, as the heart of the sturgeon still moves in its old fashion, when the blood and the whole organism has perished. We noticed this when on our asking these women whether they were Mohawks, they answered with great eagerness and emphasis, "Oh no, sir, no! No! not Mohawks—Algonquins!"

My friend and companion, who had travelled over all parts of Canada, informed me on this occasion, that the tribe of Mohawks is held in horror far and wide, even down to the present day. In a village of Mickmacks, in New Brunswick, he had noticed that they still frightened their children with the name; and that the inhabitants of a Mickmack village once actually took fright and ran ten miles, on the report that there were Mohawks coming.

The cruelties practised by the Mohawks on their neighbours must have been terrible indeed; or is the imagination of the Indians so impressible, their memory so tenacious, that after the lapse of a hundred years they are still frightened by the phantom of a race that scarcely exists any more?

I got pretty well laughed at in Canada, for having sought so anxiously, even at night with a lantern, the remains of the decayed Indian tribes? "What can you learn from these people?" it was said. "It is not worth your while. You will see nothing in them—they are the mere Canaille of the Indians. Go to the Far West, there you will find renowned races; proud fellows who look down with great contempt on their poor countrymen in Canada."

This was often said to me, and probably it was not altogether wrong; but it might be said in reply, that though the still wild and savage sons of the West had a peculiar interest of their own, which these half-tamed and often mongrel Canadians have not, yet that these mongrels often afford subjects for inquiry that the full-bloods do not. In ethnography, as in all nature, mixed and mongrel races are often specially important to the observer. Many questions can only be solved among Indians who have come more or less into contact with civilization. Of what degree of culture are they capable? To what diseases, physical and moral, are they most liable? From which do they remain free, &c.? The comparisons and contrasts with Europeans are also more easily made, and more striking, and thus the results of psychological observation are often much more surprising.

That among the savages of the West, one race should pursue another with bloody revenge and inextinguishable hatred, no one will wonder; but that this hatred should be found still burning on in the peaceful and long since Christian villages of the East, and that when its object has long since descended into the grave, this is a much more remarkable phenomenon.

I shall, therefore, not allow myself to be dissuaded from seeking out the last of the Mohawks, Algonquins, Mickmacks, and Iroquois, wherever I can find them, nor from communicating, as well as I can, the results of my observations to my readers.

CHAPTER XXVI.

THE BARRACKS HILL.

THE mass of the houses of Bytown is divided into two main groups, and between the two rises a broad-topped rock or hill, from the summit of which you command the whole position.

This rock, as well as the before-mentioned Rideau Canal, belongs to the Imperial Government of Canada, and has been taken possession of for military purposes. This hill, indeed, and many lands besides, are considered as appendages to the canal, and might help to defend it. The Provincial Government, and especially the Bytowners, would like to have this hill, which lies in the very middle of their city, and offers the finest sites for building; but though the Government might give up the Rideau Canal to the province, it will not the hills, rocks, &c., which are well adapted for military positions, and might be of importance for the defence of the town itself. Hitherto, only some barracks have stood upon this hill, and thence its name; but they presented a very miserable aspect when I saw them, as they had been almost burnt to ruins. The panorama round the hill was remarkable. The long line of the cataracts is in full view, and right and left the far-stretching buildings of the rapidly-growing "Metropolitan city of the Ottawa," and the great sluice works and other important establishments; the whole set in a background of seemingly interminable forest.

The forest is the Jupiter, and the city the Minerva, that has sprung full-grown and ready-armed from his head. The broad silvery-shining Ottawa, however —losing itself in the far distance beyond the cataracts, attracted me more than anything else. How gladly would I have followed it with more than merely the eye. There is said to be much that is interesting in that region, and it is not difficult of attainment. First, after passing the Chaudière Falls at Bytown, you come to a whole series of smaller cataracts or rapids,—the first portage, which is traversed by a fine Macadamized road. At the end of this you come to another broad tranquil part of the river, like a lake, and go on board a steamer that carries you quickly about five and thirty miles further. Then the water is again blocked up with rocks; but a little horse railroad has been made along the shore, and this brings you once more to smooth water. Near this place are the celebrated falls called the *Chats* (the Cats), but in good Canadian, the " *Choats*," and out of this the Britons have made "The Shaws;" after this you once more find yourself on a steamer—but this time a *very* small one—and then again in a carriage. You pass the long flat and fertile islands —" Calumet " and " Allumette," which will one day, like that of Montreal, be turned into gardens, but which now only serve to remind you of little travelling adventures of the Jesuits,—of the one, " Calumet," where they smoked a pipe; of the other, " Allumette," where a match suddenly gave them light and safety.

At length there opens before you the long rocky canal of which I have spoken. The Ottawa, here 350 miles from its mouth, is a broad and mighty stream, and remains such a long way further, but beyond this " Long Road " there are no vessels to be met with but the birch-bark canoes of the Indians, and no inhabitants but a few Agents of the Hudson's Bay Company, and on either side in the forest, and on the tributary rivers, the lumber-men, who make their way everywhere. But traders, mechanics, and others soon follow them. In the valleys opening from the river small stores are to be seen, from which the neighbouring country can supply its wants—and there is no doubt that many of these stores, where the lumber-men now buy their tobacco, may be regarded as germs of future Ottawa cities that perhaps before the end of the century we shall find described in our Geography books.

That it will be so may be safely assumed from the position of Ottawa, and the fact that there is no shorter natural road from Montreal and Quebec to the upper part of Lake Huron, and to the entrance of Lake Michigan and Lake Superior, than the river and valley of the Ottawa. In a short time important lines of railway will be laid down, along the Ottawa to the mouth of the tributary Mattawan, from there along the valley of this river, the shores of Lake Nipissing, and along the French river to Lake Huron. This combination of rivers and lakes is an ancient route, discovered and used by the Indians from time immemorial and communicated by them to the French Jesuits, who would not have discovered it for themselves; they would naturally have proceeded up the great channel of the Ottawa, for how could they have hit on the notion that they had to turn off to the left at the mouth of the little Mattawan, in order to reach through it the great Lakes and the most important objects and races? How could they have known that the main stream of the upper Ottawa lost itself with its sources in the cold wilderness of the Hudson's Bay countries. I repeat that our European discoveries in America rest almost wholly on the ancient explorations and discoveries of the Indians, who had tried these routes and pointed them out to our people.

The upper Ottawa, above the mouth of the Mattawan, is even to this day very little known, since it opens the way to no important traffic. Up to the year 1846 not more than half of the river had been really surveyed, and according to this survey it has been laid down on the maps as far as Fort William.

The principal merit of the further examination of this interesting stream belongs to the celebrated Canadian State Geologist, Mr Logan of Montreal, who for years together, on steamers, in bark canoes, and on horseback, has travelled with his measuring chains and compass up and down many branches of the Ottawa, to learn and describe their character and position. This excellent, amiable, and learned man has also carried the survey 300 miles further to the great Lake Temiscaming, through which the

Ottawa flows, and at the same time determined the course of several subordinate branches of the whole labyrinth.

Concerning the remote sources, which he himself could not reach, he obtained information, and had maps sent in by Indians, half-breeds, and lumber-men, which they had drawn from their own knowledge and experience. There is therefore a great deal of valuable geographical material extant for a description of the Ottawa river. One part of this material has been already incorporated with the well-known Labouchet's Map of Canada; but in the house of Mr Logan himself, and of the distinguished Mr Russel of Bytown, I saw manuscript maps with very full details, which have not yet been published.

From these maps and from the kind explanations of their owners I found what I had not expected, that a great part of the Ottawa river is still unsurveyed and unknown, although we see it on many maps very precisely laid down in all its parts. Above Lake Temiscaming it is only known to the *Gens du Chantier*, and it is not yet decided which of its branches is to be considered as the true source or main Ottawa. The true Ottawa is said to come from Grand Lake, but Grand Lake is still a hundred miles from its source.

The sources of many of the tributaries of the Ottawa, which are by no means inconsiderable, are as much lost in obscurity as those of the Ottawa itself. The great Gatineau, for instance, has been explored for 300 miles, but the 60 miles further to its springs are unknown. The Kopowa river is now being surveyed for the first time.

The maps drawn by Indians, half-breeds, and hunters of the Hudson's Bay Company are, however, not altogether to be despised. Mr Logan had the goodness to show me a map of this kind of a portion of a river, which he had received before the survey, and when he afterwards compared it with the results he had obtained by a more scientific method, it appeared that the narrowing of the channel, its angles and windings, the form and position of its islands, its lake-like expansions, &c., were laid down with wonderful fidelity. There will however soon appear some most admirable maps of Canada, on a large scale, and in these will be revealed the geological features of the Ottawa first discovered by Mr Logan, and this will be an occasion for extending still further the fame and the knowledge of this country through the world at large.

CHAPTER XXVII.

HOAR-FROST.

At midnight, on the evening when I proposed leaving Bytown, I had gone on board the steamer, and betaken myself quietly to bed in the hope of making, during the night, a considerable portion of my journey; and late the next morning when the breakfast bell raised its accustomed clamour through every corner of the vessel, I awoke, wondering not a little that I should have slept so well in the usually noisy steamer, and found that we were still quietly at anchor, and the same shore and the same Bytown lay before the windows as the night before. "What's the matter," I asked of the Canadian steward, for, to the joy of the traveller, the servants on the Ottawa, as well as the St Lawrence, are French or Canadians, that is to say, cheerful, polite, and complaisant, in fact, perfect. "*Nous nous sommes arrêtés toute la nuit, Monsieur, il fait un temps boucaneux, ce que nous appellons la brâme. Voilà Bytown, voilà les Chandieres, et tout ce que vous avez quitté hier soir.*"

Although I did not know before what a "*temps boucaneux,*" and "*ce que nous appellons la brâme,*" signified, for the words are not to be found in the Dictionary of the French Academy, I soon found it out, for, as I went on deck to see what I could see, I saw nothing, or at least only a thick fog, which did not disperse before the sun till ten in the morning. I did not regret the delay, for when at last we got into motion, I was enabled to see many parts of the river that we had passed in the night when I came. I thought I could distinguish through the still-hovering mist, the renowned Rideau Fall.

"Is not that the Rideau cataract?" I asked of an Englishman whom I saw also looking out. "No, sir," he replied, "that are Mr Mackay's water privileges." Yes, quite right, then it is the beautiful Rideau Fall,—I heard that Mr Mackay used them for a saw-mill. He has put Pegasus instead of an ox into the plough, but you should not overlook this beautiful fall, sir, that delighted the Christian missionaries 200 years ago. I had long before noticed that the word "privilege," is here used in a sense peculiar to the country; that it does not mean the privilege or permission obtained from the State, but rather the advantage that nature affords, and which may be turned to account for the acquisition of what we mean by a privilege. A Canadian Briton at the sight of a fine waterfall that might be easily applied to some useful purpose, would exclaim, "What a fine water privilege!" and in the same sense he would say, "Those privileges are become my property."

The hoar-frost or *brâme* which had settled on the trees, heightened their beauty and that of the shores in an enchanting manner. We were only in the middle of October, and the trees were still mostly covered with golden-yellow, bright-red, and dark-brown foliage with still a partial mixture of green, and the sparkling hoar-frost scattered over all these tints produced enchanting effects. The colour of the leaves gleamed through the delicate white powder, and assumed thus many new shades; sometimes it seemed as if silver dust had been sprinkled upon gold, and since the frost had settled not like snow, but gently and equally on every object, all the outlines were most perfectly defined. On the islands of the river the trees stood thickly covered with the glittering powder, and the white crystallized branches hung low down over the brown flood of the Ottawa, which reflected their image.

On the sides of the hills on the shore, all the rainbow dyes of the woods were veiled in delicate white. I thought I could never grow weary of such a lovely scene, but towards noon, when the sun had been playing for hours with these millions of crystals, his playthings began to be worn out and to disappear. He had also completely dispersed the lingering remnants of the fog that had hung for some time over the water, and from which, as our steamer passed, wild ducks and other fowl flew screaming away.

A hoar-frost of this kind had come, I was told, this year on the 1st of September, and there had been but two months quite free from frost. In general, our captain informed me, the navigation ceases about the middle of November, and the Ottawa mostly freezes over in the beginning of December, and, at least in the lake-like and tranquil portions, very smoothly and regularly, so that it mostly makes a beautiful sledge path. The transport of wood ceases then, of course, but from Bytown and from the lower part of the river come little caravans of sledges with provisions, tools, manufactured goods, &c., to supply the settlements of the lumber-men in the woods. For four or five months the river remains frozen hard and fast, and it is not free again till the beginning of April, never sooner than the 5th, and sometimes not till May, and yet under this same degree of latitude the river Gironde in France is flowing!

It is thought in Canada that the extreme cold of the climate of this country is partly attributable to James's Bay, the most southerly portion of Hudson's Bay. Into this Bay, which is without an outlet, and which stood in ill repute with the first discoverers, great masses of ice are driven by the prevailing north and north-west winds, and are there caught like fish in a net, and drive about the greater part of the year without melting; so that James's Bay radiates cold on all the surrounding country.

The most useful forest tree of Canada, the sugar maple, is also the most beautiful, at least in autumn, and developes the richest golden hue on its leaves, which also it retains longer than the other trees. Its bright hues gleamed out everywhere around us, from amidst the brown and frequently withered leaves of its neighbours. As we were going to the place where we were to make a halt, two kinds of this remarkable tree were pointed out to me, the "hard" (which is the best) and the "soft maple," from both of which sugar is obtained, but the best from the first. It yields also the best wood for fuel, and the most beautiful for cabinet work, and has indeed so many uses, that Minerva must have selected it expressly for Canada, as she did the olive for the Athenians. The sugar of the soft maple, or "plane-tree," as it is commonly but erroneously called in the country, is blacker, and does not crystallize so easily as the other. There is also a third tree in Canada from which sugar is obtained, namely, the *merisier*, or wild cherry-tree, apparently something like the "marasque" of Dalmatia, from which is made the celebrated *liqueur Maraschino*, but the sugar of the *merisier* is to be had only in small quantities, and is mostly used at the druggists' for medicinal purposes. The plane or soft maple has a white bark, with a fine silky skin-like covering, finer even than that of the birch bark. It grows on a marshy soil, and even in the water, while the hard maple prefers high and dry ground.

I had a whole council of maple connoisseurs around me, and they gave me a great deal of fresh information concerning the tree, though I had read all that had been written about it by Talbot, Hall, Buckingham, and other Canadian travellers. I am not going, however, to inflict it all on my readers.

The Canadian sugar is, it seems, obtained at the end of the winter, while the ground is still covered with snow, not like the West Indian sugar, for which the poor negroes have to be almost suffocated with heat. At the end of March, or the beginning of April, the sun gives for a few hours of the day a burning heat; this sets the sap of the tree in motion, and makes it sweet. May it not be, perhaps, the extraordinary heat of this Canadian March sun which produces sugar from the same tree that with us yields only watery sap?

When the appointed season arrives, the poor peasant families betake themselves to the woods, with pots, and pans, and ladles, and there build themselves huts, and then set about their boring operations. Sometimes they merely make a cut with the axe in the tree, and it immediately begins to weep precious tears, which are caught in basins of birch bark, and afterwards boiled in a very simple manner to a thick syrup, and, on the operation being repeated, ultimately to a solid brown crystallized mass. Since women and children, young and old, share in the labours of this sweet harvest, and find suitable occupation in it, it gives rise often to very pretty animated scenes, which, in Quebec and Montreal, you frequently see represented in pictures and engravings. They reminded me of what I had seen among the Tartar families of the Crimea, who also camp out, at a certain time of the year, to obtain a kind of syrup from their apple-trees, and also of the children and daughters of the Letts in Courland, who run into the woods in March to tap the birch-tree, and obtain its fermenting sap for household purposes. In the woods of the mountainous part of Lombardy, and the Tyrol too, they get turpentine in the same way, by tapping the pine-trees.

Fifty gallons of sap, or more, are often yielded in Canada from a single maple, and it is said without injuring the tree, which, on the contrary, grows all the better for the operation, and produces harder and better wood; but it is possible, nevertheless, to carry the matter to excess. The older and stronger the trees become, the more sap and sugar they yield. Quite young trees yield only watery sap, and it is therefore not usual to tap them till they are at least three quarters of a foot in diameter. For the discovery of this maple sugar, as for most others, the Europeans are indebted to the Indians, and in the collections of Indian antiquities may be seen the stone utensils which the ancient Indians used in obtaining it. I saw, for instance, a long stone hollowed out and pointed at the end, so that it could be stuck into the tree.

I had always imagined that this maple sugar making was an antiquated Canadian branch of industry, which was now of little importance, but this appears to be a mistake. On the contrary, the occupation is increasing in importance; it is carried on in a more regular and judicious manner, and produces every year a greater result. Large quantities of this maple sugar find their way into commerce, and a great deal is exported to the United States, where it is mixed with the West-Indian sugar, and refined with it. In Canada the maple sugar is not refined—"*Ça ne se paye pas*," but it is seen in its brown state, in which it has a certain woody flavour, in every peasant's cottage. In the more opulent families, it is used as a kind of sweetmeat, or for preserving fruit.

Since I drove through the isthmus between Grenville and Carillon, not in the stage coach, but in a little carriage of my own, I had an opportunity for examining the trees of the forest more at my leisure, and also of driving down to the shore to see the Rapids. We met a large party of Canadian raftsmen, who were passing through the forest, up the river, to make new rafts to send down, with their foreman, a great, powerful-looking man, at their head. They were all French Canadians, without any admixture of "old country folk" ("old country" meaning England). They looked very healthy and lively, showed full, round, well-fed, cheerful faces, and passed quickly by, gossiping and whistling as they went.

These people are, it is said, passionately attached to their dangerous trade, as are also the lumber-men of the forest, who prefer their occupation to every other in the world. Novices, perhaps, find it rather uncomfortable, but when they are once "naturalized to the axe" they will never again be anything but axe-men; and for this reason it is sometimes difficult in these regions to get workmen for other works, such as canals, roads, or railways. Even the Irish and Scotch, when they have been some time in the country, are very apt to make their way into the woods, join a band of lumbermen, and thenceforward earn their living by wielding the axe, possibly thinking, like Schiller's robbers—

> "Ein freies Leben führen wir,
> Ein Leben voller Wonne;
> Der Wald ist unser Nachtquartier, &c."

Between the rocks on this Rapid we saw the fragments of a raft sticking, and men busy in trying to get them out. They told us a whole "*Bond*" of twenty cribs had got wedged in here. A bond, it seems, is such a division of a raft as is sent at once down a cataract, and may consist of more or fewer "cribs." These cribs I now examined more closely. They consist of a long quadrangular frame, filled in with planks and masses of wood. The lumber-men put the frame together on the snow, launch it in the water as soon as the rivers are open, and then fill it up; and the cribs are then fastened together with ropes made of wattle.

Our journey this time was rather a land than a water one, for we found several opportunities for a walk, and towards evening were again stuck fast in a fog, and passed the night near the old French *seigneurie* of Vaudreuil, on the Lake of the Two Mountains, and I took the opportunity of visiting a German farmer, Mr Xmeier, on the shore; for, as I have said, German settlers are rather scarce here.

I found him a worthy, pleasant, and very talkative old gentleman, who, as I soon observed, was a great favourite in his neighbourhood. Everybody seemed to know "Herr Xmeier," and to like to talk to him. He was, he informed me, the son of a German soldier, who had come with the English into the country, and, like many others, had received a grant of land; and he showed me his spacious, handsome house, and his numerous and flourishing family. His son-in-law, a tall, well-grown, and intelligent man, was also a German, but had come later into the country, and had but lately sent for his aged mother and his youngest brother from the Black Forest. They had only been a year in the country, and I was amused by noticing the differences between them and the Americanized members of the family. The young

German brother had large eyes, looked modest and a little sheepish, smiled very pleasantly when you spoke to him, but had altogether the air of what people here call a "Greenhorn." He already spoke a little English, however, and in ten years' time will be doubtless as serious and self-possessed as his elder brother.

The good old mother from the Black Forest, an emigrant at seventy years of age, spoke no word of English, but sat in the corner and knitted away industriously. She was the only one in the room who was doing any work. I asked her whether she did not miss the old Fatherland, and she sighed and said she did, but that things were very different here in this fine, large house of her son's, and down there in her old cottage. "Yes, mother," broke in the son, "and you haven't got the tax-gatherers everlastingly bothering you." "Ah, to be sure," said the old lady, in the true Black Forest dialect, "there was always one or another at the door, sometimes three of 'em ringing at a time. Ah, that is true, here one has a little peace from them."

"Here in Canada, sir," said the host, "we pay almost no taxes at all, less than in the United States. Our *Seigneur* gets for ninety acres, four shillings and sixpence and $2\frac{1}{2}$ bushels of wheat. Besides that we pay a few shillings a year for the schools, and that's all. That does not hurt us much!"

On the other side from the good old mother and her knitting, two young ladies, her grand-daughters, in silk dresses, and decorated with ribbons, sat or swung themselves in rocking-chairs, with their arms folded. Some young Americans, who had come with us from the steamer, were paying court to them, and I heard French and English words mixed together, "You always talk with a double *entendre*, Mister;" "*Monsieur vous êtes un* humbug, &c."

"Children, children, how can you talk so? Have you got nothing at all to do? There you sit dressed up like the angels, and never stir a finger to do anything from morning till night." This is, I am sure, what the old grandmother from Germany would have said, but she was quite bewildered, like a hen who had hatched a brood of ducklings, and who can do nothing but wonder at their ways. Very frequently she cast a timid glance at me, as much as to say, "What must you think of these dear, naughty, extravagant, American girls?" and I had by words and gestures to give her to understand that it was only the custom of the country, that farmers' daughters here were very different from what they were in our old country, that there were advantages and disadvantages on both sides the question, &c. Taking the family group all together, however, the pretty ladylike, but certainly rather idle girls— the stout, healthy, but somewhat stupid young peasant —the industrious, saving, careful old mother, and the rather meagre but still active and erect father and grand-father, and then the absence of the everlasting tax-gatherer,—I certainly thought that, though my sympathies were with the old country, Canada had the best of it.

The rooms were very handsomely decorated with the antlers of stags, elks, and rein-deer, a decoration that with us is found only in the halls of nobles and princes, for woe to the poor peasant who should adorn his cottage in this way. The gun of the Canadian settler need make no distinctions between game and humbler animals.

"When I first came here with my father," said Mr Xmeier, "it was all forest land and full of game. We bought 160 acres very cheap, and cleared it in the course of years. Now it is clear all round, and the forest is far off. That's a difference, but look here, sir, that's a difference too," and he showed me a picture of Montreal as it was in 1803. The city really looked smaller and meaner than now one of its own suburbs, and Mr Xmeier showed me places now covered with handsome houses and churches, which were then marshy spots where his father used to shoot snipes.

Late as it was we went out in the fields to look for an old stem of a wild vine of which I had been told. It was very rough, three or four inches thick, divided into two branches, one of which had grown into a pear-tree, and the other into a maple, and evidently very old, our host thought not less than a hundred years, and therefore, though it bore little fruit, he had always respected it. Wild grapes not only grow here in the woods, but you see them twining round all hedges and enclosures like blackberries in Germany. The vine is found in the forests all up the Ottawa, that is to say, on the banks of a river which is frozen five months in the year. It seems as if the vine remembered what the latitude of the country was, though air and water have forgotten it.

The first French discoverers of the country rejoiced especially over these vines, and in their delight called, as I have said, one of the great river islands the "Isle of Bacchus." On the old maps of the St Lawrence vines and vineyards are very prettily drawn along the shores. These wild grapes too had astonished and charmed the old Northmen 800 years before the arrival of the French, and induced them to name the American country after the product that they least expected to find there, "Vineland." Those who may be still inclined to doubt of these discoveries of the old Northmen, should read in the Danish accounts the passage in which it is stated how the old German Tunker, the only German who accompanied the first Northmen to New England, came running, quite in raptures, out of a wood, with a great bunch of grapes in his hand, crying out to his companions on the shore, " Grapes! grapes! just what we have in my country." They will then see how entirely these reports agree with those of the French subsequently, who also brought, with joyful wonder, ripe grapes out of the woods of the St Lawrence.

In general, also, it is not to be denied that these cold Canadian woods abound much more in all kinds of fruit than ours do. The wild plums and cherries I have already mentioned, and besides these and gooseberries, which are very common, there are currants, strawberries, mulberries, and many others in real abundance, larger than with us, and nearly as well flavoured. "This old vine reminds me, gentlemen, that I have not offered you a glass of wine," said my old *half*-countryman, " come this way and take a glass of Rhine-wine, as good as we can offer you here in Canada. The Germans," he continued, " have a very good name in this country, and are everywhere made welcome. Here's to all Germans who may find their way to our Ottawa-land, and may they be as well content with it as I am!"

I inquired how matters stood with the Temperance movement here.

"Well," he said, "they are rather desperate with it in some places, but, for my part, I am not a Temperance man; I think every man should be his own master in such things. I, indeed, am only a German Canadian, but I like now and then a good glass of our Rhine-wine."

It was late in the night when we at last took leave of our hospitable friend, and returned to the steamer, which towards morning again got into motion, and then carried us safely to La Chine, whence we soon reached Montreal.

CHAPTER XXVIII.

THE CATARAGUI.

The name of " the St Lawrence" was first applied by the French discoverer, Cartier, to a small bay or harbour near the mouth of the great river, which was known at first as the " Great River of New France," or of Canada, as " the Great Bay," at its mouth between Canada and Newfoundland, was known in the oldest time as " Golfo Quadrado," and then as " the Great Bay of New France."

By degrees the name of St Lawrence was extended, first over this bay, which we now call the Gulf of St Lawrence, and then to the great river of Canada. This happened in the time of Champlain, at the beginning of the 17th century. During the 16th, the St Lawrence was usually drawn on the maps only to Montreal, because it was only known with certainty so far. The name remained, therefore, peculiarly appropriated to this part of the river, which also forms up to this point an undivided water channel, such as ought to be known by a single name. At the island of Montreal, however, the volume of water breaks into many different branches, amongst which the first discoverers did not for a long while find their way, so as to make out that they were only parts of two great rivers, one flowing from the north-west, and the other from the south-west. The two rivers were about equal in volume, and it was, therefore, quite natural to suppose that neither of them was the actual St Lawrence, and consequently two names were given to them; the north-western being the great river of the Ottovais (the Ottawa), and the south-western, which flowed out of a lake (the Ontario), that of the Cataragui, from an Indian village or tribe of that name.

We find, therefore, during the 17th century the idea prevailing that the St Lawrence was formed by the junction of the Ottawa and Cataragui near Montreal. Subsequently it was found that this latter remained the whole year through of more nearly equal volume than the Ottawa, and that, in fact, it was the continuation of the great body of the St Lawrence, and the name was therefore gradually extended to this part also, and that of

Cataragui entirely forgotten, so that "St Lawrence" reigns as far as the Ontario. I may perhaps, nevertheless, be sometimes permitted to use the old name for the sake of brevity, to designate the part of the St Lawrence between Montreal and Lake Ontario.

It is one of the most interesting sections of the great river, renowned for its numerous rapids, its lovely landscapes, its "Thousand Islands," as well as for its canals and other remarkable works of art. As on my journey to Ottawa the steamer first carried me to La Salle's old harbour, the often-mentioned La Chine,* and however much La Salle was mistaken in the view that induced him to bestow this name on it, he was quite right in his choice of a locality, for now, as 200 years ago, every one going upwards from Montreal in any direction, ships himself at this point. The railroads from the south and west also run to this point, this old knot of roads, and the passengers cross the river in boats. We traversed Lake St Louis along its whole length in a pretty fast-running boat, and in the afternoon reached the cataracts, by which the Cataragui pours itself into the lake. Here is again a whole series of rushing whirlpools and rapids miles long, as in many parts of the Ottawa. On many rocky reefs almost the whole river is lashed into foam, and only

* Only goods are carried by the already-mentioned La Chine canal.

a very narrow channel left free for the passage of vessels. The old French colonists distinguished three principal reefs as the *Saut du trou*, the *Saut du buisson*, and the *Rapides des Cèdres*.

These rapids, as well as the before-mentioned division of the river, favoured the idea that the St Lawrence here came to an end. The river and its name was lost in this series of cascades, and when it had collected itself again it seemed as if new born. It was from the same idea that the Romans called the Danube, below the great cataracts of the Iron Gate, not Danube but Ister.

These various "*Sauts*," or leaps, for a long time interrupted the navigation, and allowed only of the passage of small rowing-boats. In going up the river it is still necessary to make a circuit through artificial canals. In coming down, steamers venture into the labyrinth of rock and foam, since they are able better than any other craft, to move sideways or backwards as well as forwards, but even they have been only able to effect the passage within these few years. Every year, however, removes some of the rocky obstructions, and enlarges some apertures, and we heard now as we passed down exploding and thundering sounds from the shores, which gave token that the engineers were engaged in the long battle that they have here carried on against the obstinacy of Nature—a battle that they will certainly win. The passage up, by the canals, is said by travellers to be rather tedious. The steamer is locked in a dozen times, and when by the filling of its prison it is lifted to a free height, it is but to find itself, after a short run, once more in gaol. I found the operation however interesting in itself, and it seemed to be comparatively very quickly executed, especially when I considered what a great number of vessels we had met and passed. The abundance of water in the St Lawrence does indeed allow these canals to be constantly and abundantly fed, and as often as a vessel approaches, the whole series of locks are filled, without any fear of exhausting the water. The St Lawrence canals have too the advantage of never requiring to be cleaned, for the water of the river gets so purified in the lakes that it scarcely leaves any deposit.

When the distance between two sluice-gates was not too great, we passengers sometimes employed the time in taking a walk, and saw then often close to us portions of the old wild, broad, and wooded river on which Nature has not yet completed her thousand years' task.

I was told that on these canals vessels drawing ten feet of water can now be admitted, and that consequently even sea-going vessels of a tolerable size can pass them. Equally deep canals are found further up to pass round the Falls of Niagara and St Marie, so that vessels whose size and cargo is not too considerable, may now pass from Chicago, and the most distant points of Lake Superior, to Montreal, Quebec, and the Atlantic Ocean. Vessels have for some time frequently arrived at Montreal that have made an inland-water voyage of 1400 miles, and ships have been built on the Ontario to go to Australia, and sent from these harbours to sail round the world. All this seems extraordinary when it is compared with what was possible a few years ago, but greater things are anticipated. Children in America grow fast, and scarcely has a garment been made before it is found too small, and must be replaced by a larger. The Erie canal was scarcely finished before people began to talk of enlarging it and doing away with its old narrow locks. The case is just the same here. The St Lawrence canals are to be made 14 feet deep and twice their present breadth, and it is hoped the work will be completed before long, and then the larger vessels can do what only small ones can at present, take in their cargo at Liverpool or other distant harbours, and carry it what we may call up to the doors of the Backwoodsmen and the Indians.

These rapids and cataracts, as they cause an interruption in the trade, had the same effect in the colonization and political division of the country. With them terminated Old French Canada, the present province of Lower Canada. The last French villages and *seigneuries* lay on this side of the cataract and along our canal. The region is not uncultivated; on the contrary, we saw field after field stretching for miles. The old French population ceases soon on the northern shore of the river, but extends somewhat further on the southern. *Coteau du Lac* and *Longreuil* are the last French villages, and from this point begin the British Colonies and Upper Canada. The French had, indeed, many little forts and small settlements connected with them for some hundreds of miles further, and doubtless here and there cultivated lands, but the real connected and inhabited Canada of the French peasants ceases near Montreal and these rapids. Beyond this it was the Canada of the military and of the voyageurs.

Towards evening we got out into the Lake of St Francis, a broad expanse of water,—half river, half lake, such as I have described on the Ottawa,—and the night as it came on added many beauties to this imposing sheet of water that lay darkly stretched out before us, the outline of its shores being visible by light-houses and other lights. Sometimes a light would hover like a Will-o'-the-Wisp out of the deep obscurity before us, hanging in the rigging of a ship whose hull had been invisible in the thick darkness. Then a few specks of vivid light would appear on the distant horizon—fires, I was told, in the woods thirty miles off. At midnight we were again obliged to slip into a canal, and found the locks all brilliantly illuminated, and as much bustle going on on the quays and on the water as in one of our Elbe harbours in the middle of the day. The opening of the canal was full of vessels, and some pushed their way with us into the lock; and a few steamers were just rushing out of it into the wide dark Lake of St Francis.

Though we were all lit up with yellow, blue, and red lamps, we very nearly came into collision, but we did escape somehow, and when we found that the safe but tedious canal navigation, and the moving up the watery steps, began again, most of us were glad to seek our sleeping cabins, or, as the Americans say, our " State Rooms "—why so called I know not. "We have just had a narrow escape," said I to the gentleman who occupied one of the two beds in my said " State Room," as I entered. " We had very nearly ran our heads against another steamer. It is a wonder we escaped."

"Oh, yes, sir," he replied, yawning; "that is nothing uncommon in this country. The vessels are always running each other down, or blowing each other up, but we get used to it."

"Well, I do not find it easy to get used to it," said I, as I crawled into my berth.

"Oh, you must not think anything of it," said my companion—a fine young American—looking down on me, for he had the advantage of position in the upper one. "Here in Canada they are careful enough, though horribly slow. I can't stand this country, they don't go a-head enough; but you come to the Mississippi, there you will see something; there you never feel yourself safe in your berth for a moment. The boats there are very flat and thin, and such Snags as there are on the Mississippi will sometimes pierce right through the bottoms of them and stab you in your bed. Then it happens sometimes that the steamer takes fire, in a hot summer when the wood-work is all as dry as tinder, or at the time of year when they are all stuffed as full as they can hold with cotton, that catches so easily, you know—and then they and all they contain burn down to the water's edge in a few minutes.

"Sometimes, at a sudden turn, the water will run out of one boiler into the other that happens to be empty, and then it bursts, and up you go in the air.

But the best of all is the racing,—that's the way most of the vessels in the Mississippi come to grief."

"Good heavens! you are drawing a terrible picture," said I. "I will never make a voyage on the Mississippi as long as I live."

"Oh, when you are once there you forget all about it, except your imagination works itself up into a fever; and then you sleep first-rate on board one of those Mississippi steamers."

However that may be, we certainly did on this St Lawrence Canal, and when I chanced to inquire the next morning for the name of the steamer, I was told she was called the "Phœnix," and a picture of that remarkable fowl, rising from the midst of flames, hung near the entrance to the ladies' cabin. It seemed as if the ship-architect and painter had intended to console the passengers with the assurance that in case they should find themselves making a similar ascent, another steamer quite as handsome would be built again directly, and that they might transform themselves in the Phœnix style in the other world.

CHAPTER XXIX.

THE HISTORY OF A PIECE OF LAND.

THE next morning we were steaming along between Canada and the United States, for we had crossed during the night the boundary line of the British dominions, which runs along the 45th parallel of latitude. This degree separates the States of New York, Vermont, and New Hampshire on the one side, from Lower Canada on the other; and, to make the frontier plainly visible, portions of forest are cut down here and there to mark the line, and a fellow-passenger pointed out other portions of it in the night by certain lights and villages that we were passing.

This whole district, from Lake Ontario along the St Lawrence to the 45th parallel, was once in the preceding century sold to a single individual, and formed a connected domain of three millions of acres, or about 5000 English square miles. It may perhaps be interesting if I give a few details concerning this domain, as it may throw a light on the mode of distribution and disposal of land in America. They were communicated to me by a descendant of the first owner.

At about the time of the American Revolution, I do not know the precise year, a certain Mr Macomb made, with a few companions, a sporting and canoe voyage on the St Lawrence, or rather the Cataragui, and became acquainted with the great district that we were now passing, the northern part, namely, of the State of New York. It did not stand in very good repute, for it had formed part of the land of the six nations, or Iroquois, and had never been completely subjected either by French or English, but remained as a kind of neutral territory and battle-field between the two.

On the maps of the time the district is left entirely white, and it had no inhabitants but a few scattered Indians, the poor remains of the old valiant race of the Iroquois. The river Hudson and its unknown sources are pointed very variously upon it, and indeed there are in the eastern portion tracts that are not even yet thoroughly known, although it is considered with its lakes and mountains as a kind of New York Switzerland.

This sporting Mr Macomb, however, saw in it something more. He saw fine forests, useful trees, fertile fields, and fine sites for future villages and towns, and he entered into partnership with another man, and between them they raised a capital of about 200,000 dollars, with which they set about their speculation.

The financial condition of New York, as well as of all the States of the Union, was in those first years of the Revolution deplorable; the sum raised by Mr Macomb and his associate was, therefore, extremely welcome, and the Government had little objection to give in return some of their useless land, not less than, as I have said, three millions of acres, at the rate of eight and a half cents per acre—a square mile for about 50 dollars. (I have seen the original of this remarkable contract.)

The 3,000,000 of acres were then for the first time measured, and a grant made of them to Mr Macomb, or rather three separate grants of a million each. They are written upon parchment, with a great waxen seal of the State of New York appended to each. It shows on one side the sun rising among mountains; and on the other side a rock beaten by the surf, with the motto, *Frustra*. This first armorial bearing of the State has long since been replaced by another. With the territory thus acquired between Lake Ontario and Montreal, the purchasers now began land speculation on a scale that is not common even in the United States. Of course they had their district described and made known in all possible ways. They travelled to Europe to find associates and colonists; in Holland, in England, in France, they formed small companies, to which they sold portions of their land—one Dutch company, for instance, took half a million of acres; a French, I believe, a few hundred thousand, and smaller parcels were sold to private individuals.

In the mean time the original mover of the project somehow got into difficulties, and retired from the concern, leaving his partner, the ancestor of a highly-respected family in New York, as sole proprietor of the land still unsold, namely, one million of acres. He now devoted himself to getting this tract settled and cultivated, and as many of the farmers he placed on it gradually became proprietors, his million of acres had, in the course of years, much diminished; but 200,000 is still left in possession of his descendants—that is, an estate about as large as the Grand Duchy of Weimar. The present proprietor thus explained in my hearing the principles on which he has proceeded in its administration: "I let the people have my land," he said, "on very advantageous conditions, and I do not care whether they have capital or not. I desire to get healthy, vigorous men, willing to work, and of unblemished character; and these are the circumstances according to which my agents are instructed to grant or refuse applications. I leave the settler time to make himself a home in the portion of wilderness allotted to him, and to make a little profit, with which he may pay off the purchase-money. How and when he will do this depends entirely on himself, and I require no rent for the land, and no interest on the money owing me. The labour they bestow on the land is a rent they pay me; for of course until the purchase-money is paid it remains my property, and is daily becoming more valuable. This labour is in some measure controlled by my agents, and if the tenant will neither pay nor work on it, we require him to clear a piece of forest, or build a few small bridges or a barn.

" Sometimes the settler goes off, after having lived on the land ten years, without paying me a penny, but since he has left me meadows for marshes, and fields, stables, and cottages for wild forest, I find my account in the transaction, and can now sell the land for a higher price."

I saw a curious collection of maps of these extensive estates. Every township, every section was represented upon them in detail, and every single settler, and the extent of his property laid down. I noticed in running over the book that some of the properties were very small and close together: others, on the contrary, very extensive and widely scattered, and the difference was explained to me by the difference of nationality.

The small thickly-set farms belong to German peasants; the large and far-stretching ones to Yankees. The German enters timidly on this unknown country; he has no notion of helping himself so expeditiously as the Yankee does, and he always dreams of making a new home—a little Germany—wherever he is, and of being surrounded by neighbours and countrymen, and he looks out some small portion of twenty or thirty acres, that he can easily manage, and honestly pay for, and have friends and neighbours snugly settled near him.

The Yankee, on the contrary, can make himself at home anywhere; he is accustomed to do things on a large scale, and to feel himself, when at large in the fields and woods, as a true lord of creation. He has no fear of marshes or forests, but keeps to his "go-a-head" principles, and feels sure of getting on. He has no hesitation in taking a square mile of land if he can get it, or even twice as much;

then he builds for his wife and children a log-house as comfortable as he can possibly make it; and when he once has this warm nest ready, sets to work vigorously to clear his land. He does not concern himself about neighbours, he is self-reliant, and not particularly sociable, and can remain contentedly for years alone in the forest without ever coming out of it, except on business.

Very often he detests neighbours, and if they come too near him, moves off further to the West to get out of their way.

"Hills are the best neighbours," is a Yankee proverb, and even in the thinly-peopled regions of Missouri, Arkansas, &c., it is not uncommon to find farmers of even seventy years of age suddenly packing up their goods and moving away westward, for no other reason than that the country is getting too populous and "noisy" for them.

The German settlers, this gentleman said, were the most welcome to him; they were industrious and persevering, and did not wish merely to work up the land, but to make a home of it. "They are saving too, and like to lay by a little money in hard cash; they abhor debts, and it is easy to see that every dollar they pay is a weight off their minds.

"As for the Yankee, he can bear a considerable amount of debt without being at all uncomfortable;

he speculates on credit, lays out every farthing he gets on improvement, and at last very likely becomes a rich man, and pays off all at once the claim that the German has been discharging slowly, bit by bit."

CHAPTER XXX.

IMMIGRANTS.

I wish I had been acquainted with the gentleman above alluded to at the time I was making the passage up the Cataragui, for our steamer was swarming with German emigrants, all streaming towards the West, and they might perhaps have obtained what they sought without so long a journey.

The St Lawrence steamers, I was told, had been equally crowded all the summer, and every year the number of immigrants is increasing. With respect to Canada, however, they are merely birds of passage, for nearly all of them are bound for the rich prairies on Lake Michigan and the upper Mississippi.

The increase of the means of transport, the railroads, the steamers, &c., on the St Lawrence line, is probably the cause of this increase of passengers, and great efforts are being made in Montreal and Quebec to strengthen still further the Canadian means of transport. Four large new steamers have been this year placed on the Quebec and England line, and the passage is cheaper than that by New York or Liverpool. It is now possible to reach Chicago, the great central port of the West, without ever leaving the ship, and this lake and river passage offers several advantages over the long railroad journeys by Philadelphia or New York.

The belief that the immigration by the St Lawrence will now increase in an unheard-of manner is pretty general in Canada, and also that it will not have merely the transit trade, but retain some of the labour in the country.

I made it my business, of course, to observe and converse with the immigrants—for how much to occupy the understanding and interest the heart is offered by the sight of 300 people leaving Europe for America! The great majority of them too, namely, 193, were Germans, and there were 32 Swedes, 30 Dutchmen, and the rest Britons. They all looked deplorable enough, poor things! and seemed to have suffered much from the hardships of the voyage; they were very poorly clad too, and a few rather tastefully costumed Indian women, whom we had on board, were gazed at so respectfully by our German peasant lads, that if they had had to speak to them, I am convinced they would have addressed them as "Madame" or "Mademoiselle."

By the appearance of the yellow flaxen heads of the Scandinavians, it would seem that combs and brushes were scarce among them, and the babies that lay on their mothers' laps would, I hoped, some day consume more soap than had hitherto been expended on them. Germans, Swedes, and Dutch were all alike in this respect, but they looked, nevertheless, judging from their marked and characteristic physiognomies, as if something might be made of them.

The Swedes are quite a new element in the immigration, although formerly their Gustavus Adolphus did send a few of them over to the New World. Many of these our Scandinavian companions had not yet used up all the coarse bread they had brought with them from Sweden, and I saw more than one Norna-like matron take out for breakfast and dinner a large paper containing a collection of pieces of this hard bread, and distribute them sparingly to her children; and I noticed too that every little crumb that was left was carefully packed up again. I hope they have now long since been eating good American wheaten bread.

One family, in particular, I would gladly know had

thus fared. I discovered them one day, just after the luxurious breakfast that the first cabin passengers obtain on the American steamers; and then heard a second breakfast-bell ring, and a proclamation made in a loud voice that "Such of the 'tween-deck passengers as wish to breakfast, are requested to go into the cabin." This was said several times, and I was curious to see what effect this friendly invitation would have on the poor wanderers. None of them stirred, to my astonishment, at the moment, for I had forgotten that the repast would have to be paid for, and pretty highly. My Swedes remained soaking their hard crusts in a little tea, and the Dutchmen munching their bread and cheese. In the midst of the crowd, and seated upon chests and bales of goods, I saw a family group, whom I recognised at once as my country-people from the Black Forest. It was a mother and five children, who had nothing but bread and tea, without sugar, milk, or butter. I was so fortunate as to be able to procure them some of these articles, though not all, and then we got into comfortable conversation. I inquired after the place of their destination. "Mother, what's the place we're going to?" said a half-grown girl. "Ah, I don't know; father will know the name of it!" "Here, father, what's the name of the place we're going to?" and at these words came forward an elderly, serious-looking man in a long woollen coat or blouse, whom I had before noticed on the deck. The question appeared however to puzzle him a little. "What's the name of it? Well, I know there's a canal being made there down in the West, and the agent said I could work at that and get a little money, and then we could go further. But wait a bit, sir, I have it written down on a piece of paper, on the letter the agent gave me. See here, sir, it's Hamilton, that's the name of it." And hereupon he handed me a little piece of paper torn out of a pocket-book, on which was written in pencil a short recommendation of the family to an inhabitant of Hamilton. They appeared to think a great deal of this pencil-recommendation; their reliance on this scrap of paper was taking them to Hamilton.

"You see, sir," he continued, "we meant to go to Westconsin (Wisconsin), and so first to Chicago, where so many of our country-people go, but the voyage cost a great deal more than we expected. Instead of their giving us our food, and plenty of it, as they promised, we had to pay for it dearly enough, and hardly got as much as would keep body and soul together. I had to pay a shilling almost every day to the ship's cook to let my wife cook something warm for us, out of our own stores, and so it happens that I have now only got five dollars left, and the journey for us to Chicago would cost three times as much," and he showed me his five-dollar note, which, as his only treasure, he had got carefully concealed. "Do you think we shall be able to manage with that till I can earn something? You see, sir, the fact is, that I am a village doctor from the Black Forest, and I have been practising there for thirty years, but, at last, it would not do any longer; my family grew larger and my practice less, and my hair, as you see, has turned grey before my time. The people in the Black Forest are all very badly off lately, and in our village we were fairly starving. Those who have not seen it would hardly believe what I could tell them of what I have seen there."

The poor man then pulled out a bunch of papers to confirm the truth of what he had been telling me. There were his student papers, thirty years old,—the various testimonies to his having gone through a course of medical study,—the permission to emigrate from the authorities of the village, and the declaration that neither debts nor any other duties stood in the way of his intention,—good wishes that a better fate might await him in the New World, and finally his passport, and description of his person from head to foot. This passport was wrapped up with especial care, although when he had once got shipped at Rotterdam the document was not very valuable, but we Germans are brought up from our infancy with such respect for passports, that we often go dragging about the precious articles for a long time even through the wilds of America. The account these poor people gave of their voyage was terrible. They had been nine weeks out from Liverpool to Quebec, and cold and storms had brought them to the verge of destruction, and the ill-treatment they had suffered from men was worse than that inflicted by the clements. The captain and the crew had been extremely harsh, unjust, and even cruel. According to the agreement every passenger was to receive good food, but they had lain fourteen days in the harbour of Liverpool, waiting for the weather, and during all this time the captain had said they must feed themselves. He had only engaged to feed them on the high seas. For the first few days after they got to sea they used to get just enough to satisfy their hunger, but after that there were always quarrels with the Irish about the food, and the British sailors naturally took part with their countrymen, and the Germans got the worst of it. Very often there was nothing left for them, and "the Swedes and the Dutchmen were not any better off than the Germans" (I think my patriotism felt a little consolation in this). Some of these poor creatures had brought a little cheese, or bread, or sausages with them, others who had not, had to pay away their last farthing, and some, who had neither food nor money, *died and were thrown overboard*.

"Yes, sir, they died. We lost on the way twenty-seven passengers, women, children, and infirm old people who could not bear the hardships, and yet we had no cholera nor epidemic whatever on board."

"*Ja well myn Heer*," broke in a Dutchman, "seven and twenty of us died of hunger and thirst."

"Could you not complain to the captain?" said I.

"Ah, the captain, he was just the worst of all! He had no mercy on us at all, and he used to threaten to throw us overboard at once if we teased him with our complaints. He and his men treated us like slaves. The sailors used to come into our sleeping-places with ropes' ends and drive us up to work at the pumps, or some other task. Sometimes they would pour cold water over the people, as they said, to set them on their legs; and one man, who really was very weak and ill, but whom they thought well, they downright murdered. They dragged him to the deck, though he sighed and groaned, and kept pouring water upon him, to make him fit for work, they said. One night we saw him lying exhausted on the deck, and the next morning he was gone; we suppose they threw him overboard. It's a wonder we didn't all die."

"Did not you complain of the captain when you got to America?"

"Yes, and the Sanitary officers when they came on board, and found how many people had died, saw there was something wrong, and called the captain to account. He is in prison for it now in Quebec, and they say it will go ill with him."

"Perhaps it will by and by in hell," whispered a bystander to me, "but not in Quebec, I fancy; most likely the man is not in prison at all, they only tell the people these things to keep them quiet."

When I thought of what these people had suffered before they left the Black Forest, and of the purgatory this Liverpool captain had carried them through, I was grieved to know that a third time of trial awaited them in their Backwoods' life, their canal and road making, but if they could only get through this, I had little fear for their future.

I spoke with a great number of these German emigrants, and heard the story of their adventures, plans, and hopes. Many of the mechanics seemed to intend continuing their custom of wandering from place to place, even after they had landed in America. One of them, a potter, had already been in New Orleans, whence he was driven by heat and yellow fever, and also in Philadelphia, New York, and Albany, where he found the cold intolerable, and was now going to seek his fortune in Chicago. None of them interested me or occupied my thoughts so much as the poor old village doctor, and his numerous family, with his slender purse, and his scrap of a pencilled recommendation. But, unluckily, Germany was not well enough represented in the cabin to enable me to do much to help him, and Heaven knows what became of the poor creatures after all!

CHAPTER XXXI.

THE THOUSAND ISLANDS.

THE middle of that portion of the St Lawrence which, as I have said, was formerly called Cataragui, has become, I scarcely know why, the chief centre of traffic for this part of the country. The two most important towns of the district here lie opposite one another. Prescott on the Canadian side, and Ogdensburg on the American. Railroads from the interior terminate at both places, and there is therefore a great deal of life and bustle on the water. The St Lawrence is rather narrow at this point, and nowhere can a comparison be made more conveniently between a Canadian and an American town. Prescott exhibits much darker hues than Ogdensburg, where all looks brighter and pleasanter; the houses of the former are built in solid style of grey stone, the same building material that has served for Montreal. The Americans have a passion for white and green houses, and plant willows and other elegant trees between them, and the contrast might be continued to many other particulars were it worth while. You have before you at once a piece of the "old country," and one of the quite new.

Ogdensburg is the capital of the tract of land that I described a chapter or two back; some miles beyond it lies another pretty river port, Brockville, and then again some miles further begins the celebrated "Lake of a Thousand Islands;" but to have a clear idea of the origin and configuration of this lake, you must begin at Lake Ontario.

Lake Ontario forms on its western side a regularly-drawn oval, with smoothly-cut shores, and no considerable islands or appendages. On its north-eastern side, however, where its waters have broken through the obstacles that opposed their progress, its hitherto broad smooth expanse is broken up among numerous islands and peninsulas.

First comes the large peninsula of Prince Edward, then Duck Island, and several others, as well as long gulfs, bays, and inlets, breaking the land right and left. Then near Kingston you have the great Wolf Island, Amherst Island, and others; rugged masses of land that the water could not overcome, or possibly which rose above the surface when the Ontario subsided into its present bed. At length, beyond Wolf Island the lake contracts to a breadth of six or seven miles, and here begins the "Lake of the Thousand Islands." These islands are, as the name indicates, extraordinarily numerous, and the water is split up into a corresponding number of channels; but at length the river develops itself again out of the labyrinth. For a distance of thirty miles, reckoning from Kingston, the waters contract more and more, hollow out a deeper and deeper channel, and wear away more and more of the islands, which gradually become less numerous, and cease entirely some miles above Brockville. The current now becomes stronger, the two shores appear, the lake disappears, and the river takes its place; but this is for any one coming down the river, we were pursuing an opposite course.

The name of the locality, "Thousand Islands," was probably bestowed by the Jesuits, or the celebrated Canadian traveller Champlain, who was the first discoverer of Lake Ontario. The number of the islands is of course only guessed at; some make them 1500, and some as many as 3000, as they perhaps may, if they bestow the name of island on every separate bit of rock that sticks out of the water,—or every reef or sand-bank that lies just under it.

Half of these islands lie along the American shore, the rest nearer to Canada, and the frontier line has been drawn between the two, and the channel for the steamers keeps pretty closely to this line. The whole scene is renowned as interesting and picturesque both in the United States and in Canada, and parties of pleasure, pic-nics, and sporting excursions are made to it both from Kingston and Brockville. People hire one of the elegant yachts or boats built at Kingston, and sail about with their friends from island to island, dine, camp under the trees, shoot the water-fowl, fish, and amuse themselves in many ways. Many remain for days together, for the tours among these almost countless islands have something of the charm of voyages of discovery. One of the party, perhaps, declares he knows of an island that has never yet been visited; another tells of a deep, wooded bay, in whose clear, calm waters no one has yet tried to anchor.

We reached the first of the islands, a little above Brockville, and soon found ourselves surrounded by them; sometimes lying in a long string like a row of beads; sometimes flung pell-mell together in a heap. Some are large and covered with thick woods; all have trees, and there are some so small that they have only just room for one tree or a bush. There is an infinite variety in the grouping of the trees too, some being gathered into social parties, some living as solitary hermits, so that perpetually new combinations are formed in the scenery. Some of the islands are just barely hidden under a thin covering of moss and other vegetation, and sometimes the crystal water is flowing over a mass of naked rock that it barely covers.

The foundation of all these islands I believe to be granite, and in general they are not high, though picturesque pedestals are afforded for the trees by banks of twenty feet deep. The larger have hills and valleys, and arable land enough to be worth cultivating, though hitherto little has been obtained from them besides game, fish, and wood. Villages there are none, and only a few scattered dwellings or shanties for sportsmen, wood-cutters, and lumber-men, with a few mechanical contrivances, such as are seen on the Ottawa, for the collecting and transport of the felled trees. The islands all have owners, but, as everywhere in America where land, wood, and water remain unused, they have been to some extent invaded by squatters, whose huts we saw here and there on the shores, and the owners seldom offer any objection, as they consider that these people help to reclaim the land and make some steps towards its cultivation.

The best time to visit the islands is in spring and in the early summer, for then the trees and shrubs are fragrant from every cliff; the woods are full of birds and various animals; and sometimes when the air is very hot, the water is so deliciously cool and fresh that it is a delight to plunge into it. But in the cold autumn day when I visited the lake the water is less attractive; Goethe's fisherman could only have been enchanted by the Nixie on a warm summer's evening.

The autumn is, however, the loveliest time for one of the greatest attractions of the islands, and the green, red, yellow, brown, and golden leafage was beautifully mirrored in the clear water beneath. Some of the islands, when the sunbeams fell on them, seemed quite to flame, and, in fact, this does sometimes happen in more than a metaphorical sense, and the burning woods produce, it is said, a most magnificent spectacle. If you chance to be passing in a steamer, you may enjoy the sight nearer and more conveniently than a similar scene elsewhere, as the intervening water renders it safe. The boats there run very close in shore, and the passengers can look deeply into the recesses of the blazing woods and yet remain in security. I was told this by a gentleman who had enjoyed the sight; and another, who noticed the interest I took in these Thousand Islands, mentioned some further particulars. In his youth, he said, they were still inhabited by Indians, remnants of the Iroquois or Six Nations, to whom the whole north of the State of New York belonged. These islanders were called *Massassoga*, a name that still occurs in various localities on the St Lawrence; their chief resided on one of the principal islands, and the rest of the tribe was scattered about on the others, in birch-huts or tents. Their canoes were of the same material, and with these they used to glide softly over the water, and, in the numerous little bays or arms of the river, surprise the fish, which, having never been disturbed by noisy steamers, filled the waters in countless abundance. The birds and other game were equally plentiful in the woods; but now, when greedy squatters and sportsmen with guns have exhausted the district, the islands are comparatively devoid of animal life.

It was the practice among the Massassoga, at certain times of the year, to leave the islands to their young people, and make great hunting expeditions, northward into the interior of Canada, and southward to New York. My informant had visited them once when he was a young man, and being hospitably received, had afterwards repeated his visits, made acquaintance and friends among them, lived with them for weeks, and shared the joys and sorrows of the life of the hunter. Once when he had been on a journey to Niagara and the West, and had been a long time absent, he could not desist when he passed the Thousand Islands on his return to his native town, Brockville, from making a call by the way on his Massassoga friends. They recognized him immediately, gave him the warmest reception, and carried him on their shoulders to their chief, who made a great feast in his honour, and canoes full of Indians came gliding in crowds from the islands to see and welcome him. He had to pass the night among them; the squaws prepared his couch, and two of them insisted in serving him as a guard of honour at his tent door, where they camped out and kept up the fire. "I was almost moved to tears myself, sir, on seeing my half-savage friends again. Believe me, it is a race very susceptible to kindness, though, at the same time, certainly very revengeful for injuries. They never forget their friends, but are terrible and even treacherous against their enemies. We have very erroneous notions of the Indians. We call them poor and miserable, but they appear quite otherwise to themselves. They are proud of their prowess and animal daring, and of the performances of their forefathers. In fact, they think themselves the first race in creation."

"Are there now any remains of these proud people on the islands?"

"No. They have been scattered like chaff; their fisheries and their hunting became continually less productive; the villages and towns of the whites grew up around them; they began to feel the pressure of want; their race died away like the fish in their waters, and at last the few who remained accepted a proposal of the government, that they should exchange these islands for a more remote habitation,—I do not myself know exactly where."

The only living being that appeared, very common here now was the bird the English call the "loon." It is a water-fowl as large as a goose, with a very thick head and long beak; its colour black with white spots on the wings. This large bird was swimming about everywhere among the islands, and it was curious to see how exactly similar was the impulse of instinct in the numerous specimens that we met in the course of thirty miles. As long as our boat remained pretty far off, they swam quietly about on the glassy water, attending only to their own affairs, and busy in catching insects or fish; but as soon as we came within three hundred yards they shot up into the air, with their long necks stretched out, and rolling about their still longer heads, so as to look at us timidly, now with the right, and now with the left eye.

In the second stage of their fear, this anxious movement was communicated to their whole body, and they steered alternately right and left, and at last flew straight on before of us; but when they noticed that our winged steam monster was soon again within a hundred yards or so, they seemed fairly to give it up,—rolled their heads about a little more, and then threw a somersault, and went down heels over head into the water and disappeared. All these motions were repeated by every individual as exactly as if they had been previously agreed upon.

These "loons," the "wintergreens," and the numerous watch-towers among the islands, were the only objects that specially attracted my attention. This wintergreen, or *pyrola*, is a low plant or bush, that does not at all, at least in the autumn, correspond with its name—for it looked blood red, and covered the ground under the trees with a red carpet. Sometimes it ran as a border round the islands, and then the groups of trees seemed to be enclosed in a wreath of red flowers, as I have seen them in an English park. The light houses, too, tended to convey the impression that we were not upon the mighty St Lawrence, but on the artificial waters of some pleasure-ground,—for they were elegant white buildings, like pavilions or kiosks,—sometimes half hidden in a grove, sometimes rising from a little island promontory. They are numerous, and of course very necessary, as the winding watery channel is continually changing its direction in this labyrinth of islands.

By degrees—after you have breakfasted once, and had one dinner—the garden comes to an end, and you emerge upon the open field,—that is to say, the broad water, and the approach of the Ontario and the city of Kingston is announced. On the Canadian shore to the north, close along which we were moving, the houses, farms, and villages were again numerous, and on observing the dwellings closely, I discovered in some of them, to my great satisfaction, a striking resemblance to those of my worthy French Canadians of Lower Canada; the houses lie along the river as closely as there, and in the midst of them is a church—from its form and style evidently a Catholic one.

I turned to a country-looking man who was leaning, like myself, over the bulwark of the vessel, looking attentively at the houses, with an inquiry as to whether they were really inhabited by French people.

"*Oui, Monsieur,*" was the answer, "*c'est moi et mes confrères, et mes voisins, nous démeurons là depuis dix, vingt, ou trente ans. Nous sommes tous originaires du bas Canada, mais nous avons suivi le cours de l'emigration Anglaise.*"

The man whom I had addressed was a simply and cleanly dressed peasant, of very open and agreeable countenance, and modest but quite self-possessed in his behaviour. His complexion was very fresh and healthy and his aspect was good humour personified. Although he was turned of forty, he had still something youthful in his mode of speaking, and the expression of his eyes was *naïve*, I might almost say innocent. Sometimes he seemed to hesitate to speak about something, and then it seemed to me that a slight blush passed quickly across his face. His whole conversation was extremely characteristic of the true French-Canadian type.

"That is, I suppose, your Catholic Church?" said I, "*Oui, Monsieur, c'est notre petite Chapelle Française. Elle est assez grande pour nous, nous ne sommes que vingt familles ici.* Do you see there, behind the chapel to the right, that is my little abode, and all the fields behind it belong to me. That large house up there is Monsieur Jacquelin's, my cousin, he has forty acres of excellent land, and up atop of the hill there is Monsieur George, my uncle, he has thirty-five acres all nicely cleaned and dressed, fields without a stone in them, and the forest now driven a long way back. When we came here, twenty years ago, the place was nothing but trees, nothing but firs, firs, firs! we had enough to do with them at first, but now we are all well off and my property is constantly growing. I have a good wife, a daughter, and two sons. My girl has been working for some years at her *trousseau*, but I do not fear but that she will find a use for it. My two sons are both grown up, and are now away from home, employed on board steam-boats."

"Are they good and industrious?"

"Oh, sir, they are excellent fellows! Every half year they bring me punctually what they have earned. But what a good education I gave them! I had little enough myself, I barely learned to read and write, it wasn't the fashion at that time in Lower Canada. But here in Upper Canada we have very good schools, and I have taken care that my children should learn both languages, English and French, there's no getting on without the two, —I have been vexed with myself often enough for being able to speak nothing but my Canadian. It's a fine thing to learn several languages, you make yourself so agreeable to people. You see, sir, how you please me now by speaking to me in my own language, as if you were born in Canada, and how ashamed I am that I cannot return your politeness. Well, that shall not happen to my children, so I have got them a good education."

"How do you manage with the money your sons bring you?"

"I put it by for them in a good strong box—the eldest's earnings in one place and the youngest's in another. Their capital is growing every year, and the eldest has already 700 piastres. He may soon leave off travelling and come and marry and settle here. I have had my eye on a little farm for him for a long time, the piece of land up there close to my house. I have offered 600 for it, and if we put a little more to that I dare say we shall get it in time. Then my son will take a wife and come and live near us, and my second will in time do just the same, and if I cannot find anything suitable for him, I will give him a piece of my own land."

"Your children are not like the Americans then, they leave their parents to set up for themselves, and often never see them again."

"*Ah, Dieu préserve Monsieur ; je déteste ce systême là.* No! no, sir; I like to have my children all round me, like a hen does her little ones!"

All that this worthy man said may, as I before mentioned, be regarded as typical of the nation. It was all truly Canadian. The French-Canadians, in general, act and feel just like my travelling companion, who accompanied us to Kingston, and thence hastened home to his village, and to his wife and daughter, uncle and cousins.

END OF VOL. I.

www.ingramcontent.com/pod-product-compliance
Lightning Source LLC
Chambersburg PA
CBHW030302240426
43673CB00040B/1036